"Professor Stephen Kertesz, drawing on his wartime and postwar experience as a Hungarian diplomat, and using previously unpublished sources traces the clash of values and absence of consensus in the Paris Conference of 1946. He lays bare the conflicts between the Soviets, Eastern Europe and the United States which none of the negotiators were able to resolve. The absence at Paris of common moral and political values between east and west foreshadowed a series of conflicts wich were to follow. It began a process which led to the decline in trust between the Soviet Union and the West."

Kenneth W. Thompson

The Last European Peace Conference: Paris 1946 - Conflict of Values

Stephen Kertesz

The Last European Peace Conference: Paris 1946 - Conflict of Values

Hunyadi M. Mk Publishing

First edition:

University Press of America,® Inc.
(Credibility of institutions, policies and leadership; v. 10)
"Co-published by arrangement with
The White Burkett Miller Center of Public Affairs,
University of Virginia"-T.p. verso.

Second edition by permission:
1992 Hunyadi M. Mk.
Hamilton ON, Buffalo NY

Printed in the United States of America

Library of Congress Cataloging-in-Publication Data
Kertesz, Stephen Denis, 1904-1986
    The Last European Peace Conference, Paris, 1946-
conflict of values.
    1. Paris peace conference (1946) 2. World War
1939-1945 - Diplomatic history 3. World War 1939-
1945 - Territorial questions 4. Population transfers -
Hungarians 5. Population transfers - Germans
I. Title. II. Series
D814.K47 1985   940.53'14   85-7515
ISBN 0-8191-4420-7 (alk. paper)
ISBN 0-8191-4421-5 (pbk.:alk. Paper)

Table of Contents

Introduction
KENNETH W. THOMPSON

In September of 1983, the distinguished scholar and diplomat Professor Stephen Kertesz delivered a series of three lectures in Thomas Jefferson's Rotunda at the University of Virginia. The lectures as revised and the supporting documents which illustrate important policies and events make up the present volume. It contains source materials not previously released.

The University of Notre Dame Press recently published Professor Kertesz's *Between Russia and the West—Hungary and the Illusions of Peacemaking, 1945-1947.* The two volumes are complementary. They are companion studies by the Secretary General of the Hungarian Peace Delegation who refused to return to Budapest as designated foreign minister from his post in Rome at the beginning of the Communist takeover. Professor Kertesz went on to Yale University and then to the University of Notre Dame where he brought the Committee on International Relations worldwide distinction. Under his leadership, the Committee published more than sixty monographs and studies. Since then he has continued to write and publish and serve as an advisor to foundations and public agencies in the United States and Europe.

As Professor Kertesz noted, Stalin's statements concerning the new order to be established in countries occupied by the Red Army pinpointed the conflict of values between Soviet and Western approaches to the peace settlement. In the war against Napoleon, Russian troops had marched across Europe. The Tsar led Russian soldiers into Paris itself. At the Congress of Vienna, Russian ambitions for expansion were realized in the annexation of Polish territories. Having satisfied itself through the partition of Poland, the Tsarist army withdrew from other European countries. In 1945, some observers hoped that the Russians would once more show restraint. However Stalin had other plans and in April of 1945 he told Milovan Djilas: "This war is not as in the past; whoever occupies a territory also imposes on it his own social system. Everyone imposes his own system as far as his army can reach. It cannot be otherwise." (Milovan Djilas, *Conversations with Stalin,* New York: Harcourt, Brace and World, 1962, p. 114) After the epic struggle of the Red Army and given the mission of communism, Stalin envisioned the spread of Soviet authority throughout Eastern Europe. These issues came to a head in Paris in 1946.

In the core chapters of the book, Professor Kertesz opens the discussion by reviewing various peace plans put forward in what he describes as "the fog of war." Next he analyzes the patterns of peacemaking which were used in postwar conferences. Finally, he examines in chapter three the tragic fate of ex-enemy states as their interests were bargained away by others at the peace table.

The three core chapters gain added substance through the documents Kertesz includes in the study. Part I parallels and supports the first chapter on peace plans. It consists mainly of wartime statements and declarations. What emerges from these documents is the belief of President Roosevelt and some leaders in the Department of State as late as the final months of the war that a general peace conference would be held to prepare the peace treaties and a postwar settlement based on the Atlantic Charter.

Part II brings together documents which illustrate the diplomatic and political problems which arose at the Potsdam and Moscow Conferences. Kertesz gives special attention in the documents he selects to the complications caused by the exclusion of French diplomats from these conferences with their special ties to and competence on Central and Eastern Europe.

Part III is divided into three sections. Section A contains two Hungarian peace preparatory notes which proposed the creation of a cooperative state system along the Danube and preservation of the international character of the Danube River. Cavendish Cannon quoted a passage from the Danube note when the Hungarian delegation supported the Soviet dictated new Danubian convention at the Belgrade Conference in 1948. Harriman's and Schoenfeld's reports throw light on American, British and Soviet policies in Hungary.

The documents in Section B reveal the duplicity of Soviet foreign policy during the Hungarian government delegation's visit in Moscow. The pertinent secret documents, Nos. 17 and 18, are released for the first time at Professor Kertesz's initiative.

Section C combines materials concerning the Hungaro-Czechoslovak conflict and other clashes at the Paris Peace Conference. The Soviet aim was to recast the armistice agreements into peace treaties and this is what happened at the peace table. Yet for Hungary the major problem at Paris was a Czechoslovak proposal to expel 200,000 Hungarians from Slovakia. This proposed amendment to the treaty was part of a Czechoslovak policy to get rid of all non-Slavic populations. Kertesz discovered at the Quai d'Orsay a report from Prague (Document No. 20) which revealed that Deputy Foreign Minister Clementis had been convinced in August 1945 that the Hungarians from Slovakia could be transferred quickly to Hungary on the basis of an agreement with Soviet authorities in Budapest. This procedure proved not feasible and the Soviet delegation in a surprise move proposed at the Potsdam Conference the expulsion of Germans from Hungary. Henceforth the Soviet and Czechoslovak representatives argued that the Germans deported from Hungary should be replaced by Hungarians to be transferred from Slovakia.

After the First World War, Czechoslovakia acquired large territories inhabited by Germans and Hungarians. In 1945 Prague wanted to expel all non-Slavic populations. The Potsdam Conference decided to transfer the Germans from Czechoslovakia, Poland and Hungary to Germany. Subsequently, the Hungarian government was forced to conclude a population exchange agreement with unilateral benefits for Czechoslovakia. In Paris the Czechoslovak delegation proposed an amendment to the peace treaty for the expulsion of 200,000 Hungarians from Slovakia. It became the major task of Kertesz and his colleagues at Paris to defeat the Czechoslovak amendment. Documents Nos. 26 and 28 are reports of Kertesz's conversations with General Pope of Canada and P. Costello from New Zealand. They illustrate the pro-Czechoslovak feelings of many of the conference participants. Document 29 is a review by the late Philip E. Mosely of volumes published by the Hungarian Ministry for Foreign Affairs on Hungary and the Conference of Paris.

Thanks primarily to American support of the Hungarian position, the conference rejected the Czechoslovak amendment. Kertesz's article (the last item in the book) on "The Expulsion of the Germans from Hungary" is the only scholarly source of a dismal chapter of postwar diplomacy concerning the interaction of Soviet and Western representatives and an example of the struggle between Communists and Smallholders on foreign policy questions.

The Last European Peace Conference: Paris 1946 is the well-documented story by a participant of an early chapter in the Cold War. It reveals a persistent problem: the lack of consensus and common values between East and West. The Paris Conference was the first public confrontation between the wartime allies. Kertesz who was to become a leading intellectual figure in international relations in the United States retained a calm detachment then and has continued to held such a view into the 1980s. It is appropriate that we begin consideration of consensus and policy with this case study in relations between the Soviet Union and the West.

Documentary Sources
For Chapters I to III

Planning for Peace in the Fog of War

When we speak of "peacemaking" after major wars we think of great congresses, like those of Westphalia (1648), Utrecht (1713–14), Vienna (1814–15), and the Conference of Paris after the First World War. Such solemn meetings sought to establish lasting peace, shape new political, territorial, and juridical orders. The Second World War was the first major conflagration in modern history which was not followed by a comprehensive peace settlement. Peace preparations in the United States and in most belligerent countries assumed the convocation of a general peace conference at the close of hostilities. Yet the expected conference remained in Never-Never Land. Peace treaties were not concluded with the leading Axis powers, Germany and Japan. The Charter of the United Nations was signed in June 1945, but—unlike the Covenant of the League of Nations—the new world organization was not part of a peace settlement.

During hostilities preparations for peace are taking place in foreign offices, through diplomatic channels, conferences, and last, not least, in battlefield. The Department of State began to prepare for peace in 1939. In the following year a department memorandum explored the "consequences to the U.S. of a possible German victory." Later peace preparations took on a more optimistic tone. There seemed three categories of postwar problems— establishment of an international organization of universal scope, economic and financial policy reforms, and plans for a peace conference.

Peace preparatory work was successful in establishing the United Nations and in economic and financial matters. The International Monetary Fund and the World Bank created by the Bretton Woods agreements in 1944 secured monetary stability and economic growth, and together with GATT, increased trade in the industrialized world and helped the developing nations. Officials in the Department of State who prepared position papers for the peace negotiations assumed that the United States would possess overwhelming military and economic power at the close of hostilities and that the peace making would be influenced by the Four Freedoms and the Atlantic Charter. They looked to democratic independent countries west of the Soviet Union.

But the State Department did not participate in high level decisions during the war and had little influence on the course of events. By and large it was restricted to routine diplomatic activities. Ambassador Charles Bohlen testified some years later before the Senate Committee on Foreign Relations that the State Department had no representatives who ever sat with the Joint Chiefs of Staff or the President. "In that sense, the war was run very much from the point of view of the military considerations." Bohlen explained that while he was an assistant to Secretary of State Edward R. Stettinius, Jr., one of his duties was to serve as liaison officer with the White House. He was appointed to this position at the end of 1944 because Roosevelt's confidant, Harry Hopkins, had come to realize that "it was a very dangerous thing for our purposes to have the Department of State so completely out of the picture." We may note that Loy Henderson, George Kennan and other specialists in Russian affairs did not participate in decision-making during the war.

When we discuss wartime policies, we must remember that the Western democracies were not prepared politically and militarily for the great struggle in 1939. Although the United States had about two years for military preparations, an American military force satisfactory for a two-ocean war did not exist at the time of the Japanese attack. Until July 1944, British troops in Europe and the Far East outnumbered the Americans.

Between 1941 and 1945 at least two wars were fought simultaneously, one in the Far East, the other in the Atlantic. The war in North Africa and the Mediterranean was an introductory phase of the European war. There had been interactions between these wars, a competition for soldiers, sailors, weapons, landing craft and other things. These factors influenced wartime decisions and ultimately the preparation for peace.

Roosevelt's concern after Pearl Harbor was to mobilize the country's resources, build ships, and train a huge army for battles in the Pacific and Europe. Meanwhile, it was necessary to support Britain's and Russia's warmaking abilities through Lend-Lease, and foster fighting spirit. Loss of either country would have postponed victory into an uncertain future. Most general staffs in Europe and America estimated that the Soviet army would collapse in a few months. In this period it was in American national interest to give military aid to the Soviet Union. But even in the post-Stalingrad era Lend-Lease was not used as a means of diplomatic pressure. In 1942 and 1943, it was rightly suspected in Washington and London that Stalin was considering an arrangement with Germany for a separate peace.

A grand design for Western strategy was worked out by Winston Churchill during a voyage to Washington in December 1941, and the subsequent Arcadia Conference in Washington established the top military organ of the American-British war effort in the form of the combined Chiefs of Staff Committee. A comparable committee for political affairs was not created. Roosevelt decided that military considerations should prevail during the hostilities and political and territorial questions be submitted to a peace conference. It is true that without military victory political ideas usually do not prevail, no matter how wise. But Roosevelt's approach gave the military a role for which they were not prepared. As Karl von Clausewitz put it, "The act of war in its highest point of view is policy, but of course a policy which fights battles instead of writing notes." He added that "General experience teaches us that, in spite of the great diversity and development of the present system of war, the main outlines of a war have always been determined by the cabinet; that is, by a purely political and not a military organ." This consideration was not followed in Washington.

Contrary to the American approach, Stalin had political objectives in mind from the outset. When Foreign Secretary Anthony Eden visited him in December 1941, he demanded immediate recognition of the Soviet Union's expanded boundaries as defined in the Nazi-Soviet deal in August 1939. He proposed other territorial changes in Eastern and Central Europe, and was prepared to support acquisition of bases by Britain in western European countries. Stalin proposed the division of Europe into Russian and British spheres of influence. He wanted territorial clauses in the

Anglo-Soviet Alliance treaty signed in London in May 1942, but the clauses were omitted because of American objection. At this stage of the war a second front in Europe and increasing Lend-Lease deliveries were more important to Stalin than a promise for the future.

Stalin's demand for a second front in France coincided with the desires of the American military leaders, who from the beginning advocated a massive invasion of Europe across the English Channel because it was the shortest route to Berlin. General George C. Marshall and his colleagues at an Anglo-American military conference (July 26, 1942) proposed the occupation of Cherbourg in the autumn of 1942, a preliminary move to a general attack in 1943. The British argued that there was no hope of Anglo-American forces still being in Cherbourg by the next spring. The American Chiefs of Staff reported back to the White House and Roosevelt instructed them to agree to some operation that would involve American forces in action against the enemy that year. The conferees decided on an invasion of French Northwest Africa, which had been part of Churchill's grand design.

In the African theater General Bernard L. Montgomery defeated General Erwin Rommel's forces at El Alamein in early November 1942, and a few days later an Anglo-American landing at Casablanca, Oran, and Algiers succeeded, despite some French military resistance and political complications. Churchill and Roosevelt met in conference near Casablanca in January 1943, and decided to exploit the success in Africa by invading Sicily, securing the line of communication in the Mediterranean, and intensifying pressure on Italy in expectation of an early Italian surrender. Roosevelt announced the much debated "unconditional surrender" principle, to the joy of the Nazi propaganda minister, Joseph Goebbels. This principle weakened the possibility of an uprising against Hitler, yet it informed the world of American and British determination to fight until destruction of the enemy.

Although the misfortunes of war delayed military operations in North Africa, events in Italy were speeded by the Anglo-American invasion of Sicily (July 10, 1943). King Victor Emmanual dismissed Mussolini (July 25) and appointed Marshal Pietro Badoglio as prime minister—who announced continuation of the war but really wanted to change sides. The Mediterranean strategy was to separate Italy from Germany, and the stage was set for this policy. The

Allies expected Italy's surrender, but no realistic political or military plans had been prepared for so favorable turn of events. A document prepared by an Allied committee in London assumed that an Italian government that decided to capitulate could do so without German opposition. This assumption was sharply contradicted by reality. At the time of Mussolini's dismissal only scattered German forces were in Italy and the Germans planned to defend a line north of Pisa and Rimini. Because of blunders, illusions, and misunderstandings between the Italians and the Allies, the surrender was signed only on September 3 and proclaimed five days later. The Italians had no idea of the weakness of Allied forces. While Badoglio believed he was deceiving the Germans and was secretly bargaining for favorable terms, the Germans sent 19 divisions to Italy. The tricky operation of changing sides in the middle of the war succeeded, but Italy became a battlefield for almost two years.

While the uncoordinated United States and British policies had harmful effects in the Mediterranean, the victories at Stalingrad and Kursk changed the conciliatory Soviet attitude in 1943. The political implication of Soviet military successes was recognized in Washington. Roosevelt told Cardinal Spellman in early September 1943 that most of Europe would become a Soviet sphere. In the American perspective Danubian Europe remained primarily a British concern, although later in the armistice agreements and at the Yalta and Potsdam conferences American responsibility was assumed. Military victories increased Russian self-assurance. Moscow used the Katyn affair for severance of diplomatic relations with the Polish government-in-exile in London (April 29, 1943), and Soviet policy was forcefully expressed at the Moscow Conference of Foreign Ministers (October 18–November 1).

The American hope for peace was based on a new security organization, to provide for worldwide cooperation. Secretary Hull submitted this plan with enthusiasm to the Moscow Conference of Foreign Ministers. Ambassador Robert D. Murphy, General Eisenhower's political advisor, rode with him from Casablanca to Algiers and was astonished to discover that "the veteran Tennessee politician had become fascinated with the possibilities of establishing close, friendly relations with Soviet Russia." Murphy noted that Hull was "virtually co-creator with the President of the 'Grand Design' for the postwar world, a plan which assumed that the

United States and Soviet Russia could become partners in peace because circumstances had made them partners in war."

At the Moscow Conference a Four-Power Declaration on general security meant acceptance of the principle of a world organization. Secretary Hull rightly considered this triumph important for American diplomacy. The three governments agreed "that Austria, the first free country to fall a victim to Hitlerite aggression, shall be liberated from German domination."

Despite such declarations, the trend at the Moscow Conference had been ominous for the future of the small states west of Russia. Eden was compelled to withdraw his proposal permitting federations in Europe. Molotov argued that such a plan reminded the Soviet people of the *cordon sanitaire* directed in the past against the Soviet Union. Abandoning a long-standing British policy, Eden agreed to the immediate conclusion of a Soviet alliance with Czechoslovakia and to President Eduard Beneš's visit to Moscow. A few weeks later Beneš signed a treaty of mutual assistance in Moscow. This meant that Stalin had a reliable ally in Danubian Europe.

The Moscow Conference was followed by the Teheran meeting of the Big Three at the end of November 1943, characterized by a manifest intimacy between Roosevelt and Stalin. On Stalin's invitation Roosevelt moved into the compound of the Soviet Embassy and the two men had their first meeting without Churchill. Roosevelt went out of his way to please Stalin in condemnation of France and other matters, and according to Charles Bohlen, some of his statements showed ignorance about the Soviet Union.

The fate of Danubian Europe was foreshadowed at Teheran when Stalin persuaded Roosevelt that from Italy the maximum number of troops should be sent to southern France and he proposed that this invasion take place two months before the invasion of northern France. General Marshall and Admiral Ernest King agreed with Stalin's views but suggested that D-Day be the same for both operations in France, and the conference accepted their proposal.

At Teheran Stalin politely endorsed Roosevelt's ideas concerning a postwar security organization and the Big Three agreed in vague terms that Poland's boundaries should move westward. This meant abandonment of the American principle that territorial questions should be settled at the peace conference.

Between Teheran and Yalta decisive military actions took place. The all-important Overlord, the landing in Normandy on June 6, 1944, proved a great success, and Anglo-American forces advanced rapidly and soon controlled large areas, while Mediterranean strategy was restricted to slow-moving military operations in Italy. The finest Western divisions had been assigned to Overlord and transported from Italy to England before the end of 1943.

General Henry Maitland Wilson, the Supreme Commander of the Mediterranean, foresaw as far back as March 1944 the unavoidable delay of the landing in southern France and reported that the best way to help Overlord was to abandon any landing on the Riviera and concentrate on Italy. Occupation of the Istrian peninsula would have made feasible a push through the Ljubljana Gap toward Vienna and the invading Western armies could have attacked German troops from the flank and moved in the direction of Hungary. Such British proposals in the summer of 1944 were rejected by General Eisenhower and President Roosevelt.

Eisenhower's British political adviser Harold Macmillan commented that a break through the Ljubljana Gap and march into Austria "might have altered the whole political destinies of the Balkans and Eastern Europe." He concluded in melancholy: "Thus were sown the seeds of the partition of Europe, and the tragic divisions which were destined to dominate all political and strategic thinking for a generation."

Meanwhile events were moving rapidly. In August 1944, King Michael of Rumania surrendered to the Russians, appointed a new government of national unity, and declared war on Germany. As soon as the Soviet troops reached the Danube, Moscow declared war on Bulgaria in early September without notifying London and Washington, while the British and Americans were negotiating an armistice with the Bulgarian government in Egypt. Then the Soviet army occupied Bulgaria without firing a shot, and the armistice negotiations were transferred to Moscow.

In view of the advance of Soviet troops, and of Western strategic decisions, Churchill tried to secure British influence in the Balkans, primarily in Greece, by negotiating with Stalin and offering him controlling influence in Rumania. After preliminary negotiations and a tentative agreement in the summer of 1944, Churchill and Eden visited Stalin in October. Churchill expressed in percentages the influence that Britain and Russia should have in specified countries. In Churchill's dramatic narrative it appeared that Stalin accepted without discussion the percentage figures Churchill proposed for Rumania, Greece, Yugoslavia, Hungary and Bulgaria. Yet release in 1973 of the secret British records throws new light on Churchill's presentation. In the course of a long discussion Stalin recognized overwhelming British influence in Italy and Greece but claimed in the case of Bulgaria the same 90 percentage influence as in Rumania. Eventually they agreed that Eden and Molotov would work out an agreement on Bulgaria.

The Eden-Molotov meetings were complicated by the Bulgarian armistice negotiations and Soviet proposals to change the percentages in the case of Bulgaria, Hungary, and Yugoslavia, in favor of Russia. Molotov and Eden during long argumentative sessions advocated a variety of percentages for Bulgaria, Yugoslavia, and Hungary, and concessions were combined with power in the Allied Control Commission (hereafter ACC) in Bulgaria. Eventually Molotov offered a compromise of 80-20 percentages in favor of Russia in Bulgaria and Hungary and 50-50 percentages in Yugoslavia.

The British were satisfied with the compromise. Eden noted on October 11 that "We obtained what we wanted on almost all points. I should say 90 percent overall. In particular they will summon Bulgars out of Greece and Yugoslavia tonight." The last point was most important for Britain because Soviet advance in the direction of Athene and Istanbul seemed possible.

At the outset Stalin preferred coalition governments in the occupied countries instead of a direct Communist takeover. This is what he tolerated in Rumania and Bulgaria for a short time, and for a longer period in Hungary and Czechoslovakia. The government in Poland was handed over directly to reliable Communist Poles. The West probably lost credibility and suffered a political and moral defeat when Britain and the United States did not intervene forcefully to support the Polish uprising in Warsaw, for on this occasion Stalin showed his hand; the Soviet army stopped at the gates of the city, for political and military reasons, and Stalin refused to permit refueling of Western planes at Soviet airfields; the Western powers were unable to send substantial supplies to the Poles fighting under desperate conditions from August 1 to October 2, 1944. Lack of Western determination and guts must have encouraged Stalin.

All this was a prescription for disaster in Eastern Europe.

Developments in the autumn of 1944 made clear what was in store for the Danubian countries and Poland if not for the whole of Central Europe. Secretary Hull realized that the Soviet Union was not carrying out the cooperation agreed upon at Moscow and Teheran, and asked Ambassador Harriman in Moscow the reason for the changed Soviet attitude. Harriman replied that "when the Russians saw victory in sight they began to put into practice the policies they intended to follow in peace."

When the Big Three met at Yalta in February 1945 the Western armies had hardly recovered from the German blow in the Ardennes and the Soviet army was sweeping through Poland and had reached the Oder, and it occupied most part of Hungary. The military situation created a favorable negotiating position for the Russians. Stalin agreed again to lofty principles. The State Department had prepared a Declaration on Liberated Europe, which promised democratic governments established through free elections. The declaration at first had been combined with a proposal for a four-power Emergency High Commission for Liberated Europe that was to supervise the application of the declaration. But Roosevelt decided to present only the declaration, which the Russians accepted. Correct application of its principles might have made possible democratic institutions in the East European countries.

In the case of Poland and Yugoslavia, East and West at Yalta backed rival governments, and so it was decided that the Communist-dominated provisional government of Poland should be reorganized "on a broader democratic basis with the inclusion of democratic leaders from Poland itself and from Poles abroad." A similar recommendation was made in the case of Yugoslavia. The Curzon line was slightly changed in favor of Poland and recognized as the Soviet-Polish border. The conference also recognized that Poland must receive substantial accession of territory in the north and west and that the final delimitation of the western frontier of Poland should "await the Peace Conference."

Zones of occupation in Germany were approved. These zones, including Berlin's anomalous position, were not results of shrewd Soviet diplomacy; they were proposed by a British cabinet committee in 1943, approved later by the United States and the European Advisory Commission, and accepted by the Russians at Yalta. Churchill noted that in 1943 "a common opinion about Russia was that she would not continue the war once she had regained her frontiers, and that when the time came the Western Allies might well have to try to persuade her not to relax her efforts."

To make sure of a timely Russian intervention against Japan, Roosevelt negotiated with Stalin a secret agreement in which the United States promised to support territorial concessions to Russia in the Far East. On the last day of the conference Churchill was informed of the agreement and he signed it grudgingly.

Thanks to Churchill's efforts, and Roosevelt's change of mind, Stalin reluctantly accepted France as one of the occupying powers in Germany and Austria and as a member of the Allied Control Council in both countries, but the French zones were carved out from the zones assigned to Britain and the United States.

The sequence of events demonstrated that the settlement of fundamental issues were not postponed to a peace conference. Decisions made at the Moscow, Teheran and Yalta conferences, the armistice agreements and the military occupation zones shaped postwar Europe. The handwriting was on the wall at the time of the Teheran Conference, but the Western leaders, primarily President Roosevelt, concentrated on military priorities. General Deane, a member of the American delegation at Teheran, noted:

> Stalin appeared to know exactly what he wanted at the Conference. This was also true of Churchill, but not so of Roosevelt. This is not said as a reflection on our President, but his apparent indecision was probably the direct result of our obscure foreign policy. President Roosevelt was thinking of winning the war; the others were thinking of their relative positions when the war was won. Stalin wanted the Anglo-American forces in Western not Southern Europe; Churchill thought our postwar position would be improved and British interests best served if the Anglo-Americans as well as the Russians participated in the occupation of the Balkans.

In dealing with the Soviet Union, a multinational imperialistic great power, a country that respected military power more than the principles advocated by the West, one has to recognize that fatal misunderstandings had affected Western policies throughout the war. It is part of human affairs that the American, British, and Russian historical background influenced the result. So did Roosevelt, Churchill, and Stalin and their respective states of health. In summit conferences clear agreements were made in military matters, but important political questions remained in limbo. Usually the Soviets gained immediate advantages and made gestures with acceptance of vague principles. Since there were no Anglo-American joint policies, Stalin had a field day at tripartite meetings. Eden considered him a superb negotiator and noted: "He never wasted a word. He never stormed, he seldom was even irritated."

Relations between the Big Three and their tactics at summit meetings influenced policies. The fact that on some occasions Roosevelt and Churchill competed separately for Stalin's cooperation had not been helpful for Western interests. The President was fond of Churchill and after September 1939 they exchanged more than 1,700 letters, telegrams, and other messages and participated in eight bilateral meetings, in addition to the Teheran and Yalta conferences with Stalin and conferences at Cairo with Generalissimo Chiang Kai-shek and the President of Turkey, Ismet Inönü. Yet Roosevelt considered the leader of the British Empire as a representative of a bygone world of nineteenth-century colonial imperialism, and was convinced that the United States and Russia must get along in the postwar world. At Teheran he thought that Churchill and Stalin were competing for influence in the Balkans and told his son Elliott that he saw "no reason for putting the lives of American soldiers in jeopardy in order to protect real or fancied British interest on the European continent." Both Roosevelt and Churchill were convinced that each could get more from Stalin through direct personal contact than through tripartite negotiation.

Spectacular Western military successes during the last stage of the war were not used for political purposes. General Omar Bradley said in his memoirs concerning British insistence that the Americans occupy Berlin before the Russians: "As soldiers we looked naively on this British inclination to complicate the war with political foresight and non-military objectives."

President Roosevelt's sudden death meant that Harry S. Truman assumed the nation's highest office with a broad historical background and sound political instinct but next to no knowledge of the Roosevelt-Churchill-Stalin meetings, inter-Allied agreements, and other wartime decisions. He was not involved in White House discussions on foreign policy and not informed of such an undertaking as the Manhattan Project. It was a failure of the Roosevelt administration that the vice-president did not receive systematic briefing. The time span of less than three months between inauguration day and Roosevelt's death is an explanation but not an excuse of this omission. On April 12, 1945, the day Truman became president, he noted in his diary, "I knew the President had a great many meetings with Churchill and Stalin. I was not familiar with any of these things and it was really something to think about but I decided the best thing to do was to go home and get as much rest as possible and face the music." Lack of political purposes during the war was followed by Western passivity during the immediate postwar period. President Truman continued policies established by the Roosevelt administration, despite changed circumstances, and the American military leaders in Europe were impressed by the Russians. A few days before the Potsdam Conference General Lucius D. Clay, second in command to Eisenhower for German affairs, told Bohlen that "the key to getting along with the Soviets was that you had to give trust to get trust."

The sudden demobilization of the American army in 1945–46 changed drastically the power equation. There was an almost irresistible popular desire to bring home the boys and return to normalcy. General Marshall had to carry out this policy, and his predicament was truly pathetic. In the early autumn of 1945 he asked the journalist Marquis Childs to see him, and Childs noted the conversation:

> Disbanding the 7 million Americans under arms with reckless haste meant abandoning vast military stores, he said. Supplies worth billions were being bulldozed under the earth or dumped into the sea. What I am to do? he asked. This is an advertisement to the world that we are giving up our positions of strength everywhere.

Marshall commented later on the result of demobilization and told an audience at the Pentagon that when as secretary of state he attended the Moscow conference of Foreign Ministers in March 1947 he was urged constantly by radio messages to give the Russians hell.

> At that time, my facilities for giving them hell—and I am a soldier and know something about the ability to give hell—was 1 and ⅓ divisions over the entire United States.

This is quite a proposition when you deal with somebody with over 260 and you have 1 and ⅓. We had nothing in Alaska. We did not have enough to defend the air strip at Fairbanks . . .

A distinguished diplomatic historian, Raymond J. Sontag, pointed out some years ago that during the months between the Second Quebec Conference of September 1944 and the Potsdam Conference of July–August 1945 the United States attained a peak of strength unparalleled in American history. During the same period "the decisions were made which were to place our country, and the Free World, in a mortal peril which continues to this day." Then Sontag developed his thesis, that "despite clear evidence of Soviet bad faith and Soviet ambitions . . . and despite the warnings of the Acting Secretary of State and our Ambassador to the U.S.S.R., the positions of strength were abandoned, and the western world placed in mortal peril: Why?"

To this question historians have given a variety of inconclusive answers. There might be truth in the allegations that Roosevelt's increasing illness in 1944–45, wrong military estimates concerning Japan's military capabilities and intentions, played a role at Yalta. But the Yalta agreements, and especially the unassertive Western policy in 1945, cannot be explained by such factors. Roosevelt's health could have made the difference in decisions of lesser importance, but Yalta as a whole was the logical result of the wartime policy of the Western powers, their military weakness at the outset, and neglect of postwar problems in wartime diplomacy and at summit meetings. As a prominent member of the American establishment, John J. McCloy, put it: "We concentrated so heavily on the actual conduct of the war that we overlooked the need for political thinking." Whether this or that was decided at Yalta or elsewhere in the closing period of the war was of little consequence in view of the absence of Anglo-American determination to reestablish a reasonable European system and check Soviet expansion. Disbanding the American army in an unsettled world was a symbol of lack of policy.

After the Second World War a constructive peace settlement was not in the cards. In addition to wartime strategy and policies and the resulting military situation at the close of hostilities, a major stumbling block has been the conflict of fundamental values between the Soviet Union and the Western allies. East and West had different ideas about the meaning of wartime declarations, and particularly about the meaning of democracy, freedom, human rights, and the structure and purposes of the society of states. At the Congress of Vienna in 1814–1815 and at the Conference of Paris in 1919, the values of the major victorious powers were roughly the same and their vision of the future was compatible. This was not the case after the Second World War.

Postwar Patterns of Peacemaking: The Potsdam, Moscow, and Paris Conferences

After the Second World War an unprecedented method of peace-making began. As noted, peace treaties were not concluded with major enemy states, Germany and Japan and an internationally recognized status quo, a political and juridical order was not established. Western states signed a peace treaty with Japan in 1951, and the Western and Communist countries later concluded patchwork agreements with the two Germanys, but this tortuous procedure was a poor substitute for a comprehensive peace settlement — the declared purpose of American foreign policy under the Roosevelt administration. Conclusion of peace treaties was restricted to five less important ex-enemy states. The plan for a major peace conference was not abandoned explicitly but rather unwittingly with the acceptance of a gradual approach to the conclusion of peace.

At the Potsdam Conference of the Big Three in July 1945, the American delegation proposed and the conference accepted the establishment of a Council of Foreign Ministers (hereafter CFM) of the five principal victors: the Soviet Union, the United Kingdom, the United States, China, France. It was agreed that in discharge of this task each treaty should be drafted by the states which signed the armistice with that particular enemy. For the Italian settlement France was to be regarded as a signatory to the armistice. This meant that Britain and the Soviet Union prepared the treaty for Finland. For the three Danubian countries it was Britain, the Soviet Union, and the United States. For Italy, France and the Big Three. Here was the origin of the 4-3-2 formula of peacemaking. Western expectation was that the Council of Ministers at an initial meeting would agree on basic issues and their deputies would cast the agreement into comprehensive form, and draft the details and provisions of lesser importance. At a second meeting the Council would consider these drafts and decide controversial questions. Texts prepared by the Council would be submitted to "the United Nations," and their recommendations would be considered by the Council when approving the final version of the five treaties. The French Government accepted the invitation to participate in the CFM and emphasized that France was "interested in all important questions concerning Europe in any region of Europe. This applies particularly to the settlements concerning Rumania, Bulgaria, Hungary and Finland."

As to the origin of this scheme, Secretary of States James F. Byrnes noted in his memoirs that he thought at the time of the Potsdam Conference that a start should be made promptly and he hoped experiences with the "less controversial five peace treaties" would make it easier to agree on Germany's problems. He supposed that after agreement on certain general principles of the five treaties, the Foreign Ministers would take up the German treaty, agree on fundamental problems, and then appoint different deputies to draft a German settlement. The peace treaties then "would be presented to all the United Nations for considerations and amendment." Byrnes contemplated that a similar course would be followed later for Japan. When the meaning of the reference to the United Nations was discussed at Potsdam, Stalin remarked that the inclusion of such a phrase in the document made no difference as "the three powers would represent the interests of all." Byrnes had assumed "that at the end of hostilities an era of peace would be so deeply desired by those nations that had fought the war in unity that the inevitable differences of opinion could be resolved without serious difficulty." In this spirit Byrnes believed that the peace treaties could be prepared in a few months.

The gradual approach to peacemaking might have worked in the nineteenth century and even after the First World War because the leading Great Powers had the same view of the world and their aspirations and expectations were compatible. But the Western and Soviet vision of the political and juridical order to be established by the peace settlement differed greatly. In the war against Napoleon, Russian troops had marched over Europe, and the Czar himself had arrived in Paris with his army. But at the subsequent

Congress of Vienna, Russian ambition had received satisfaction with Polish territories, and the Russian army withdrew from other European countries. Although Western nations hoped in 1945 that the Soviets would imitate this precedent, Stalin had no such intention.

The Potsdam scheme was favorable for Soviet design because four out of five ex-enemy states were located in the Soviet sphere. Even the piecemeal approach could have been improved at Potsdam with the inclusion of Austria. The Moscow Declaration of 1943 had recognized that Austria was an occupied country to be liberated and a state treaty with Vienna should have preceded the conclusion of peace treaties or should have been concluded simultaneously with them. This procedure should have made possible the simultaneous evacuation of foreign troops from Italy and the Danubian countries. At the time of the Potsdam Conference the United States power position was overwhelming. Stalin understood the meaning of power and could have been persuaded to accept the primacy of the Austrian treaty. But President Harry S. Truman's major concern was at Potsdam to secure Soviet intervention against Japan. With rapid American demobilization at the close of hostilities, the power equation in Europe drastically had changed.

The expectation for a speedy conclusion of the five peace treaties proved to be an illusion. The first session of the CFM met in London in September 1945, and ended in three weeks without accomplishing its task. The Council was unwilling to consider some far-reaching Soviet aspirations in Japan, the Mediterranean and the Balkans and Molotov retaliated with procedural demands that the other participants could not accept. After this failure, the definitive pattern of peacemaking was worked out in December 1945 at the Moscow meeting of the foreign ministers of the United States, Britain, and the Soviet Union. The Big Three resolved that draft treaties prepared by the CFM on the basis of the 4-3-2 formula should be submitted to a conference consisting of five members of the Council and sixteen other Allied nations that had fought in Europe with substantial contingents. The conference was to meet in Paris not later than May 1, 1946, to discuss the draft treaties, express opinions, and make recommendations. The Soviet government had opposed a peace conference with wider jurisdiction and would have preferred a peace settlement exclusively by the Big Three. After the conference rituals, the Council was to establish the final text of the treaties and forward them to the other victorious and ex-enemy states.

It was decided at the insistence of the Western governments that opportunity should be given to the ex-enemy states to discuss the treaties and present their views at the Paris Conference. France was particularly anxious to avoid even the appearance of dictation, in view of the experiences after the First World War. French diplomacy and particularly President de Gaulle resented that France was not invited to participate in the Yalta and Potsdam Conferences. After Potsdam elaborate notes and negotiations were necessary to satisfy France and secure her participation in the Council of Foreign Ministers. Insult was added to injury when in November 1945, Secretary Byrnes proposed the convocation of the Moscow conference on the basis of the Yalta agreement which provided for periodic meetings of the foreign ministers of the Big Three. Reports of French ambassadors from Washington, Moscow, and Prague reflected French dissatisfaction with the American arrangement which automatically excluded France from the Moscow Conference. These reports reached de Gaulle's desk and possibly fostered his anti-American feelings. Yet, at the request of the Moscow Conference, France accepted to host the Peace Conference, and during the CFM meetings and at the Paris Conference, French diplomacy played a leading administrative role with skill, grace, and dignity.

The Deputy Foreign Ministers began their deliberations in London in January 1946, and the Council of Foreign Ministers had two sessions in Paris. The United States proposed in February 1946 that the Austrian treaty be prepared along with the five peace treaties and Byrnes submitted a treaty draft to the CFM in April "For the Reestablishment of an Independent and Democratic Austria," but Molotov was unwilling to discuss it. Byrnes argued politely, but did not insist and the occasion was lost. When the CFM decided that Italian sovereignty should be restored on the conclusion of peace and consequently foreign troops should be withdrawn, Molotov reluctantly agreed to withdraw troops from Bulgaria.

In the Council of Foreign Ministers the Soviet delegation returned to wrangling on procedural matters. Time-consuming Soviet tactics exasperated the Western delegations. Ambassador Bohlen mentioned that on one occasion the British Foreign Secretary

Ernest Bevin, became so irritated when Molotov attacked Britain for past sins in international affairs that he

> rose to his feet, his hands knotted into fists, and started toward Molotov, saying, "I've had enough of this, I 'ave," and for one glorious moment it looked as if the Foreign Minister of Great Britain and the Foreign Minister of the Soviet Union were about to come to blows. However, security people moved in . . .

The Council examined thoroughly boundary disputes outside the Soviet zone, such as the controversy between Yugoslavia and Italy. Both countries wanted Trieste, a port on the Adriatic. Both governments argued their cases before the Council four times. There were hearings on the Franco-Italian and Italo-Austrian boundaries, in addition to spot investigations of all three boundary disputes affecting Italy. Even Australia, New Zealand, and the Union of South Africa presented their views to the Council concerning the Italo-Yugoslav boundary quarrel. While Italy was permitted to present its case orally before the Council, similar requests by other ex-enemy states were turned down.

Eventually the Council reached agreement upon a large number of treaty articles. The Soviet delegation insisted that the conference could not be convoked before agreement on all treaty clauses. The American delegation argued that the Potsdam and Moscow conferences had charged the Council to prepare treaty drafts and submit them to a conference of Allied nations, but complete draft treaties were not required. As soon as agreement was reached on Italy's reparation deliveries to the Soviet Union, the Soviets agreed to set the opening date of the conference for July 29. This was another example of a procedural objection dropped when the Soviet Union received a concession. There remained twenty-six points upon which members of the Council could not agree. Disagreement on procedural questions still delayed the sending of invitations to the conference. The Soviet delegation opposed dispatching invitations until the Council had accepted the Soviet draft of conference procedure. Byrnes argued repeatedly that the Council could not impose rules of procedure on an assembly of sovereign states. Molotov insisted that conference recommendations be made by two-thirds majority. Eventually a compromise was reached; draft rules of procedure—enclosed with the invitations—suggested decisions of the conference by a two-thirds majority vote. Secretary Byrnes emphasized that the suggested procedural rules did not represent a hard-and-fast agreement comparable to agreed treaty clauses—an essential distinction because the Foreign Ministers agreed to support at the conference the treaty clauses they accepted in the Council. The Soviets were convinced that the only important task of the Conference of Paris was prompt approval of the Council's agreements.

Delegations of twenty-one nations at long last assembled at the Luxembourg Palace by the end of July 1946, and the participating states were: the United States, United Kingdom, Soviet Union, France, China, Australia, Belgium, the Byelorussian Soviet Socialist Republic, Brazil, Canada, Czechoslovakia, Ethiopia, Greece, India, the Netherlands, Norway, New Zealand, Poland, the Ukranian Soviet Socialist Republic, the Union of South Africa, and Yugoslavia. Separate representation of the Ukraine and Byelorussia was in accord with the Yalta arrangement where Britain and the United States promised to support a proposal to admit to original membership in the United Nations these two Soviet Socialist Republics.

Machinery of the conference consisted of a General Commission, a Legal and Drafting Commission, Military Commission, five Political and Territorial Commissions, and two Economic Commissions—one for Italy, and the other for Finland and the three Danubian countries. Five Political and Territorial Commissions had representatives from those nations actively at war with the enemy states concerned. In these commissions Communist states and non-European countries prevailed. Members of the Hungarian Commission were the United States, United Kingdom, the Soviet Union, France, Byelorussia, the Ukraine, Australia, Czechoslovakia, India, New Zealand, Canada, the Union of South Africa, and Yugoslavia.

At the conference debates on procedure continued for more than a week. The majority of delegates opposed the Council's proposal that required a two-thirds majority for a recommendation and agreed on majority decision. Byrnes and Bevin supported the majority's desire to allow the conference to make recommendations to the Council by two-thirds vote or by majority. After long argumentative sessions this motion was accepted by a 15-to-6 vote; the "Slav bloc" (Soviet Union, Byelorussia, Ukraine, Poland, Czechoslovakia, Yugoslavia) voted against it, and Molotov accused Byrnes and Bevin of violating Council agreements. Byrnes explained again that there was no obligatory agreement on procedural questions and announced that at the forthcoming meeting of the Council the United States would support any recommendation accepted by two-thirds vote even if the American delegation voted against it at the conference. Subsequently the conference accepted fifty-three recommendations by two-thirds majority and forty-one by simple majority.

On Secretary Byrnes' proposal the press was admitted to all meetings of commissions and the plenary sessions, an unfortunate innovation in peacemaking for most speakers addressed their remarks to public opinion in their own country and some sessions became unproductive examples of public diplomacy. In the United Nations propaganda speeches are boring and ineffective but usually harmless rhetorical exercises, but the Paris Conference of 1946 had to discuss issues to be settled by treaty provisions.

The conference had a narrow focus, and it was almost out of context if a delegate brought up constructive ideas. Herbert V. Evatt of Australia introduced several amendments to bring the treaties more in line with concepts of peace and justice. Among them was the establishment of a European Court of Human Rights that could have given realistic meaning to treaty clauses on human rights and fundamental freedoms. The proposed court could have extended protection to minorities under alien rule. Evatt proposed commissions to study territorial disputes. Such proposals were in harmony with American thinking, but the United States delegation voted against them because of a Council agreement. Molotov accused the Americans and British of being behind amendments he did not like, apparently believing that the United States controlled small states in the same fashion as he controlled the "Slav Bloc." Reasoned discourse between the two blocs seldom was possible. Quiet diplomacy facilitates compromises but was rarely used in Paris; propaganda speeches at open meetings had the opposite effect; once a public stand is taken, it is difficult for governments to make concessions. Open meetings widened the gulf between East and West.

The Soviet idea about peacemaking was simple: Moscow wanted to transform the armistice agreements into peace treaties. Molotov made clear that he considered the armistice agreements as final settlements and proposed that the peace treaties confirm them.

The noncooperative Soviet attitude stirred crises and blocked serious negotiation. A member of the American delegation, Philip E. Mosely, remarked retrospectively that "in negotiation of this kind the most reluctant government determines the maximum rate of progress." It was a great Soviet advantage that the Danubian ex-enemy states were under Soviet occupation; only Italy was outside the Soviet sphere. In this bewildering atmosphere even minor Soviet concessions brought relief. Fundamental problems were avoided, and participants limited the issues and range of discussion. Most delegations were in a hurry to attend the General Assembly of the United Nations in New York, postponed from September 23 to October 23. The CFM decided that the closing session of the conference should be on October 15. Byrnes and Molotov in a private meeting agreed on a simplified procedure for the forthcoming plenary sessions and Byrnes inquired what Molotov thought would be done "if despite all efforts the conference had not voted on all questions before it by October 15." Molotov said the work "must be finished by that day." Byrnes raised the possibility that the work would not be finished. He recognized that Molotov wanted to return to Moscow before coming to New York but felt that "if absolutely necessary the conference should stay in session a few days more in order to complete its work." Molotov repeated that "they should make sure that the conference complete its work by the fifteenth." This is what happened.

A British observer of the Paris Conference of 1919, Harold Nicolson, was present throughout the Paris Conference of 1946. He was a veteran of the British foreign service and had devoted his life to the study and practice of diplomacy and characterized the pace of negotiations as follows:

> It is the way of every conference to begin like a tortoise and to end like a greyhound. But no conference that I have ever attended showed a greater disparity of progress between the commencement and the finish. During the first six weeks the Conference dragged itself along painfully at the rate of an inch an hour; during the last four weeks there was a breathless scramble to conclude. In frantic haste the delegates rattled off their final speeches, the concluding votes were registered in an indecent rush, and so anxious were the statesmen not to miss the *Queen*

Elizabeth that there was no time at the end for the cus-
tomary courtesies and farewells.

The final text of the five peace treaties was drawn by the third
session of the CFM in New York in November–December 1946. At
the outset Molotov's cordial and cooperative attitude seemed to
show he was satisfied. Then for weeks he repeated Soviet proposals he had offered at previous meetings, and disregarded the
recommendations of the Paris Conference. During the fourth week
of the exasperating New York session in a private meeting he asked
Byrnes what could be done to make progress and Byrnes replied
that since Molotov had rejected practically all recommendations
of the Paris Conference he saw no hope to agree upon the treaties
and nothing remained but to admit failure and disband. Molotov in
bewilderment said Byrnes was unduly pessimistic and asked him
not to take hasty action and observe developments at the next
meeting. Because Moscow had much to gain by concluding the
treaties, Molotov then reversed his policy and at subsequent meetings "handed out concessions like cards from a deck." The Council
approved forty-seven of the fifty-three recommendations adopted
by two thirds majority at the Paris Conference and twenty-four of
forty-one adopted by simple majority.

Here was another demonstration that Molotov under pressure
reversed inflexible policies and the sudden volte-face raised
the question of lost opportunities because of lack of Western
assertiveness.

In postwar planning it probably was a major mistake to conclude peace treaties with the five less important ex-enemy states
before concluding a treaty with Austria and reaching at least a
policy agreement on Germany. The German question was by far
the most difficult issue for the Western democracies and Russia,
but an agreement on its solution should have created better conditions to tackle less difficult problems. The assumption that conclusion of peace with the lesser ex-enemy states would help the
settlement of the German question was an illusion because it
disregarded the nature and purposes of Soviet foreign policy.

One of the consequence of the Potsdam schedule of peacemaking
was postponement of the major peace conference *ad Graecas
Calendas,* and this meant shelving if not burying a basic policy-
assumption of the Roosevelt administration. Peace preparations in

the State Department had assumed that a major conference would follow hostilities. This plan was replaced by a piecemeal approach and this change was favorable for Soviet designs. Little give-and-take was possible because four out of five ex-enemy states were in the Soviet sphere.

If Moscow would not have accepted a reasonable order of peacemaking, the Western powers could have concluded a separate peace with Italy, as they did with Japan in 1951, and the British and American sections of the ACC would have remained in the Danubian ex-enemy countries. In this way the West could have preserved a bargaining chip lost by conclusion of peace treaties. In the framework created by the Potsdam and Moscow Conferences, the Western powers were primarily interested in consolidation of Italy's international position. Nominal sovereignty was of little value for states in the Soviet orbit. Independence of Hungary and Rumania remained fictitious because the peace treaties authorized the Soviet Union to keep unlimited forces in those countries for maintenance of lines of communication with the Soviet army in Austria.

During the period between the Yalta Conference and the Japanese surrender, the United States was the strongest world power, but at the time of the Paris Conference of 1946 the demobilized Western nations had only weak occupation forces in Europe, and more importantly, lacked political will to make a meaningful European settlement. They wanted to finish an unpleasant business in Paris. Even in this mood Western peacemaking was less than satisfactory. Despite Soviet occupation of the Danubian region and the presence of a strong Soviet army in Central Europe, it was frustrating to witness the overcautions attitude of Western delegates. Wartime concessions to Moscow were understandable. But at the peace table only determined resistance to unjustified Soviet demands could have a result. There were exceptional delegates—like Evatt of Australia, but their proposals were from voices in the wilderness. The approach of the Western Great Powers was similar at best to the old Austrian policy of *weiterwursteln*—muddling through.

The monotonous repetition of Soviet demands throughout the negotiations in the Council and at the Paris Conference was far different from the Atlantic Charter and the Declaration on Liberated Europe, documents endorsed by the USSR. Elevation of public discussion to a higher level might not have impressed Molotov, but would have provided appealing and uniting ideas for the public opinion of countries participating in peacemaking. Separate handling of issues coupled with separate votes in Commissions and plenary sessions of the Paris Conference, without reference to overriding principles proclaimed in the war years, offered a chance for a field day for Molotov.

The peace treaties signed in February 1947, implicitly gave the stamp of legality to the Soviet position established in Eastern Europe at the close of hostilities. The gradual seizure of power by the Communists in Hungary in 1947, incorporation of Czechoslovakia into the Soviet sphere in February 1948, and exclusion of the Western powers from the Danube by the Russian-dictated Danubian convention signed at the Belgrade Conference in the same year—all these were logical consequences of wartime and postwar policies.

Ex-Enemy States at the Peace-Table

The status of the delegations of defeated countries was more liberal in 1946 than after the First World War. In 1919, the German and later the other ex-enemy delegations were invited to Paris to receive the peace treaty completed by the victorious powers. They were permitted to deliver only a formal address and submit written observations. During their stay in Paris, they were confined to their headquarters which was under military control. They were not permitted to have any contact with the outside world unless they received in each case special authorization from the military commander.

In 1946, delegations of the five ex-enemy states were allowed to present their cases at plenary sessions of the conference and later, by invitation, before commissions and subcommittees. Unlike the Paris situation in 1919–1920, they enjoyed full freedom of movement and could visit delegations participating in the conference and any other diplomatic mission in Paris.

The French Foreign Ministry had assigned hotels and the Hungarian delegation's headquarters was in Hotel Claridge on the Avenue des Champs Elysées. We lived there with the delegation of the Union of South Africa, the chairman of which was Field Marshal Jan Christiaan Smuts, who had participated in the peace conference after the First World War. With this background, he was one of the most experienced statesman in international affairs at the Paris Conference in 1946. I had several pleasant and informative conversations with him. He understood our predicament, but the influence of the Union of South Africa and the other far away countries was minimal at the conference.

Since our hotel was not a secure place for discrete meetings, thanks to a private arrangement, I could use the apartment of a distinguished French family to establish contact with members of delegations participating in the conference. At the Hungarian legation a close friend handled the invitations. It was necessary for me to meet privately representatives of victorious powers who were interested in Danubian problems and Hungary's affairs. On one occasion I did not accept Molotov's invitation for lunch he gave to the Hungarian delegation because ranking diplomats had already accepted my invitation for the same time to this apartment.

Members of an ex-enemy delegation could attend conference sessions only when invited; they were not negotiating partners, but played roles comparable to those of defendants in criminal proceedings. However, the members of an ex-enemy diplomatic mission accredited to the French government and newspapermen from ex-enemy countries, could attend all plenary meetings and commission and subcommittee sessions of the conference. This was an unprecedented innovation. For the first time in history all negotiations took place before the public eye at a peace conference. But the impact of publicity was counterproductive in some cases.

I will characterize briefly the position of four ex-enemy states at the peace table and subsequently will discuss more extensively the problems and actions and experiences of the Hungarian peace delegation.

The interests and policies of the ex-enemy states differed greatly. The Allied powers recognized Italy as a co-belligerent in October 1943. She was occupied by British and American troops and enjoyed Western support. Although the peace settlement affected the fate of many more people in the Soviet-occupied Danubian countries than on the Italo-Yugoslav border, the Trieste area became one of the most contested issues at the peace table because Trieste was on the border between the Soviet and Western zones. At the conference Italy was the only country that declared war on France.

Among the Danubian countries, the Rumanians were self-confident because they enjoyed all-out Soviet support. The army had followed King Michael's order when Rumania changed sides suddenly in August 1944; the new government declared war on Germany, and Rumanian divisions fought alongside Soviet troops. The government of Petru Groza, installed under Soviet pressure by the end of February 1945, was Communist dominated and Rumania had ceded Bessarabia to the Soviet Union. All these events might have influenced Soviet policy in the conflict between Hungary and Rumania.

Bulgaria, as Germany's ally, had been at war with Britain and the United States but had maintained diplomatic relations with the USSR during the war. As soon as the Soviet troops occupied the Rumanian shores of the Danube river, Moscow declared war on Bulgaria in early September, followed by a peaceful march of Soviet troops into Bulgarian territory and transfer of the armistice negotiations with Britain and the United States from Egypt to Moscow. The Soviet Union emerged as the main actor in Bulgarian affairs. A new Bulgarian government declared war on Germany and the Soviet Union recognized Bulgaria as a co-belligerent. In the fight against Germany, Bulgarian troops lost about 32,000 men. In view of these events and the historically strong pro-Russian feeling in the country, Bulgaria expected forceful Soviet support at the peace table. The Bulgarian Minister to France, Ivan Marinov, informed me that his government was not going to sign the peace treaty unless Bulgaria received access to the Aegean Sea. The peace treaty did not give the Bulgarians any satisfaction on that territorial claim.

Finland's case was uniquely complicated. At the end of November 1939, Soviet troops attacked Finland and the Kremlin established a "democratic government" of Finland, members of which were Finnish Communists living in exile in the Soviet Union. During the following hundred days of the Winter War the world admired the heroic Finnish resistance. But admiration alone without effective support had not been helpful against the overwhelming military power of the Soviet Union and the Finnish government concluded peace on Soviet terms in March 1940. Finland ceded more territory than those occupied by the Soviet army during the hostilities. In August 1940, the Finnish government, following Sweden's example, permitted German troops to pass through Finland to Norway and in June 1941, using this transit right, German troops were concentrated in Finnish Lapland. After the German invasion of Russia, the Soviet air force began attacking Finnish territory and the government in Helsinki declared that Finland was at war with the Soviet Union. But Finland fought for national purposes and refused to participate in the offensive against Leningrad or the Murmansk railway. The Finnish army occupied Soviet Karelia and territories ceded to the Soviet Union. Despite this restraint, under Soviet pressure Britain declared war on Finland in December 1941. In 1943-44, Finland tried to extricate itself from the war and several complicated negotiations took place with the Soviets and the Germans. Eventually, an armistice agreement was signed in Moscow in September 1944, which reconfirmed the peace treaty of 1940 with numerous important changes and additions.

The Finns thought at the outset that they might argue their case seriously at the peace conference. Prime Minister Mauno Pekkala had arrived with three cabinet ministers, leading representatives of political parties, and a galaxy of experts, prepared to negotiate any questions connected with the proposed peace treaty. Pekkala went with members of his delegation to the press gallery at the first session of the Political and Territorial Commission for Finland. Although it was an open meeting, their group was asked to leave, but Finnish journalists were permitted to stay. The Finns realized the nature of the conference, and most of the delegation returned to Helsinki, Foreign Minister Carl Enckell, remaining with a few officials of the Foreign Ministry.

During the armistice period Finland was the only ex-enemy country free from foreign occupation. Its geographical location was less important from the Soviet point of view than those countries situated on the highway to Central Europe or to Istanbul. Although at the Paris Conference Britain and the five Commonwealth countries were members of the Political and Territorial Commission for Finland, this setting was sheer formality. The Finnish treaty was prepared by the Soviets. When I visited Finland's envoy to France, Johan Helo, he told me his government would accept the peace treaty without much opposition, implying that the Finns were not in a position to resist Soviet demands.

In the plenary session of the conference, the foreign minister of Finland pointed out that cooperation with Moscow was the basis of his country's foreign policy. Yet he asked for modification of territorial clauses of the treaty and made a mild plea for a one-third reduction in the $300 million reparations. Molotov saw no reason for changing the treaty and pointed out that Finland had not been occupied, implying that—unlike the Danubian countries—Finland had not had to bear occupation costs and other inconveniences of military occupation.

One may conclude that delegations of the ex-enemy states came to the Paris Conference with a variety of political predicaments, aspirations and expectations. In view of their divergent interests they had hardly any contact with the other ex-enemy delegations. As noted, they were excluded from conference session, except when invited and did not participate in the diplomatic life of the French capital.

My personal situation was exceptional. Although I was Secretary General of the Hungarian Peace Delegation, as minister-counselor to the Hungarian legation I was accredited to the French Government, and consequently enjoyed all privileges of resident diplomats and was invited to French and other diplomatic receptions. From the French point of view, I was not representative of an ex-enemy state. Yet my favorable position did not alleviate our operational difficulties which included belated notifications from the Conference secretariat. On one occasion the notification was delivered after the deadline. Our delegation often had to prepare memoranda and addresses in French and English within a very short time. I protested in such cases, but the secretariat could not be blamed. The conference wasted precious time on procedural and other inconsequential debates and only a limited time remained for discussion of questions of substance. The secretariat simply carried out instructions. As soon as the commission chairmen realized how little time remained for substantive questions, the procedure became speedy if not erratic and the ex-enemy countries were at the bottom of the totem pole. Our operational problems were aggravated by the lack of space for our secretariat because the Claridge was overbooked and part of our archives remained at the Hungarian legation.

But technical inconveniences appeared insignificant in comparison to our difficult political situation. Within a lifetime Hungary had appeared for the second time as a defeated country at peace negotiations following a world war. In the First World War the major ally of Austria-Hungary was the German Empire, which was declared undemocratic and imperialistic. But in the Second World War, Hungary was considered a junior partner of Hitler's Germany, and the Nazis had committed horrendous crimes well-publicized after the war. We would have liked to discuss the circumstances of our involvement in the war, but such topics could not be clarified. The Paris Conference debated the draft of the peace treaties prepared by the CFM. Responsibility for the war and for wartime behavior was hardly mentioned. We had submitted a memorandum on Hungary's responsibility, and hoped it would be read and discussed. But responsibility for the war was not debated; perhaps such discussion was not desirable. The Soviet Union had negotiated the Molotov-Ribbentrop Pact of August 1939, which made possible the German *Blitzkrieg* against Poland.

In this difficult situation the Hungarian delegation had to find ways to present Hungary's international problems and at the same time defend the vital interests of the nation. An important part of this task was to protect the mistreated Hungarian population in neighboring states. Our peace preparatory notes discussed the pertinent questions and proposed measures for correction of intolerable situations.

The origin of this problem was the peace settlement after the First World War which shifted large territories with over three million ethnic Hungarians, that is almost one third of the Hungarian nation, to neighboring states. It was not possible to turn back the wheels of history, but we proposed a constructive reorganization of Danubian Europe. Our peace preparatory notes were addressed first to the victorious Great Powers, and later to the Conference of Paris. These notes disapproved the antagonistic inter-state relations in Danubian Europe and emphasized the need of close economic and cultural cooperation and political reconciliation of neighboring nations and made specific proposals in these fields. These "peace aim" notes posed the general problems of Danubian Europe in constructive terms, advocating regional economic reorganization, freedom of navigation on the Danube and revival of international control over the river, deemphasis of narrow nationalism, institutionalized cultural cooperation, "spiritualization" of frontiers, self-determination of peoples and an effective system for the protection of national minorities. The Soviet envoy in Budapest, Georgij Pushkin, expressed dissatisfaction with the Hungarian proposals and this was understandable. Soviet policy was not the reconciliation of nations but to "divide and rule" in countries under Soviet occupation.

It was obvious that the Kremlin had a clear line of policy toward the Danubian countries from the beginning of Soviet occupation and Hungarian diplomacy could not have changed it, no matter what we did in 1945–46. The defeat of the Communist party at the Hungarian elections in October and November 1945 baffled the Soviets and probably delayed the Communist seizure of power at least by one year, but did not evoke the Kremlin's sympathy for Hungary.

It was an exceptional phenomenon at the peace table that a country in the Soviet zone requested support of the Western powers concerning questions in which Moscow was following a different policy. Since in such matters there were no secrets in Paris, I thought it advisable to inform the Russians personally about our objectives. I visited the Soviet embassy several times before the opening of the conference and talked with Alexander E. Bogomolov and Fedor T. Gusev, ambassadors to the French and British governments, respectively, and with A. A. Lavrishchev, head of the Southeastern European Division in the Soviet Foreign Ministry. I outlined Hungary's political and economic problems, emphasizing our conflicts with Czechoslovakia and Rumania, and described our proposals for reorganization of the Danubian region on the basis of self-determination. I received polite, stereotyped answers, mainly about the general purposes of Soviet foreign policy. This was a graceful form of evasion. On one occasion I reminded Bogomolov of Lenin's doctrine of self-determination of peoples and quoted Lenin's severe criticism of the Versailles Treaty and argued that a genuine Danubian settlement should be made on the basis of self-determination of all nations. Bogomolov introduced his lengthy, philosophical, but entirely negative answer with the statement that principles have only a relative meaning. Conditions change. What seemed just and true after the First World War may no longer be true, he said. While Gusev appeared to be a reserved and taciturn Russian type, Bogomolov was more outgoing and willing to argue. Lavrishchev belonged to a younger generation and he was educated entirely by the Soviet state.

The Soviet diplomats received me always in the same room at the embassy where most probably our conversations were recorded. It was easier to have interesting discussions with them around a dining table, but they accepted social invitations only in groups. On one occasion Lavrishchev politely accompanied me into the corridor of the embassy and I invited him to have lunch with me. He became embarrassed and could hardly mumble an evasive answer. French colleagues were amused because they had similar experiences with Soviet diplomats.

We did our best to smoke out the Russians, but real human

contact did not develop on any level, although even Foreign Minister Molotov was friendly and sometimes cracked jokes at diplomatic receptions. On social occasions liquor made communication with Soviet diplomats easier, but smalltalk was of no consequence. A lunch the Hungarian envoy to France, Paul Auer, gave at the legation in honor of the Soviet delegation was instructive. As usual in the course of such contacts with Russians, everybody had to join in the toast game, that is, each participant had to toast a member of the other delegation and after several drinks the atmosphere was rising. As the round of toasts were delivered, my assignment was to greet Lavrishchev. I expressed hope that his work would contribute to peaceful and cooperative relationships in the Balkan peninsula and referred to the role of Balkan problems in European politics. Molotov, my vis-à-vis at the table, laughed in a slightly inebriated state, while pounding the table with his glass and saying cheerfully, "The Balkans, the Balkans are very important." Deputy Foreign Minister, Vyshinsky in his toast emphasized that we should forget bygone unpleasant aspects of Soviet-Hungarian relations and talked in glowing terms about the promising future of Soviet-Hungarian friendship. Remembering that at conference sessions he had strongly attacked Hungary's case, when the clinking of glasses subsided, I could not help remarking to Molotov that "Pilate also washed his hands." Molotov burst into laughter and retorted, "Young man, be careful, there are dangerous comparisons."

My neighbor at the table, Bogomolov, was in a more relaxed mood than any time I saw him at the Soviet embassy. Apropos Vyshinsky's friendly toast I related to him a story about the famous Hungarian playwright, Ferenc Molnár, who met by chance in the washroom of a hotel the critic who had published an unfavorable review of the premiere of Molnár's play. The critic started to apologize and praised the play, saying that he had a bad headache, felt miserably, and left after the first act and had to write the review at home in a hurry. Next day he read the play carefully and was most favorably impressed. Molnár replied, "This is fine. But I hope next time you will praise my play highly in the newspapers and criticize it in the washroom." Bogomolov was amused by the story, and suddenly began to make allusions to some phases of my career. Among other things, he mentioned my Rockefeller fellowship at Yale in 1935–36 and in Oxford and Geneva in the following year.

Apparently his purpose was to let me know that he had a file on me. Perhaps his disclosure was a warning.

When we visited the Ukrainian and Byelorussian delegations, the reception was friendly, the hospitality first-class, the discussion long and frustrating and the result from our point of view negative. We received a lot of information about their suffering during the war. What they said was true enough but did not alleviate our problems. The heads of the Ukrainian and Byelorussian delegations were not professional diplomats. They were talkative and colorful people and ranking Communists. They informed us about the Soviet position in very different surroundings from those of the diplomats of the USSR. We would receive an appointment at the Byelorussian delegation at 9:00 P.M. The head of the delegation, Kuzma V. Kiselev, would receive us courteously and offer seats around a white dinner table where he was sitting with his advisers. First he offered a variety of cold cuts, exquisite fruits, cheese, then plenty of vodka. When we characterized the plight of Hungary and suggested a substantial reduction of our reparation payments, Kiselev described in detail the suffering of Byelorussians during the military operations. He said that entire villages were destroyed and people still lived in caves and dugouts. After a long discussion of Hungary's and Byelorussia's problems, we left empty-handed. Dimitrii Z. Manuilsky, head of the Ukrainian delegation, handled us in similar fashion. Such was the usual result of our visits at Soviet headquarters.

By the time the conference convened in Paris, the Council of Foreign Ministers had already formulated most provisions of the peace treaties and the members of the Council were obligated to support them at the conference table. This rule was not favorable for Hungary in connection with our territorial claim on Rumania. Transylvania had been a major bone of contention between Hungary and Rumania during the war and in the armistice period. Despite Soviet encouragements given to postwar political leaders in Budapest and to a Hungarian government delegation in Moscow, concerning Hungary's territorial claim in Transylvania, at the London session of the CFM in September 1945, the Soviet delegation was unwilling to consider an American proposal to study the possibility of a modest revision of the Hungarian-Rumanian boundary along ethnic line. The negative Soviet attitude was the same at the meeting of the deputy foreign ministers a few months later. The Soviets simply refused even to discuss the possibility of returning to Hungary some ethnic Hungarian territories along the Hungarian-Rumanian boundary. In view of the unyielding Soviet opposition, Secretary Byrnes, in a period of East-West concessions in May 1946, proposed in the CFM the reestablishment of the Trianon boundary between Hungary and Rumania.

Thanks to American support, it was still possible to bring up at the conference the Hungarian-Rumanian boundary question. On August 31, 1946, in a joint session of the Hungarian and Rumanian Political and Territorial Commissions, envoy Paul Auer delivered an address. In view of the negative decision of the CFM and in harmony with a private American suggestion, he asked the reattachment to Hungary of only 4,000 square kilometers along the boundary; this would have meant reattachment of approximately a half million persons—about two-thirds of whom were Hungarians—and with them some major cities along the boundary. Auer emphasized the necessity of international protection of Hungarians remaining in Rumania. The Foreign Minister of Rumania, Gheorghe Tatarescu in a speech at a joint session of the Hungarian and Rumanian Commissions on September 2, opposed Auer's proposals for the revision of the Trianon boundary. Even if Hungary could have obtained majority support, the Paris Conference had no power to change the unanimous decision of the Big Three.

The greatest direct threat to Hungarian interests at the Paris Conference was a Czechoslovak proposal for the expulsion of 200,000 Hungarians from Czechoslovakia to Hungary. Since the Czechoslovak proposal was an amendment to the draft treaty accepted by the CFM, only a unanimous approval of the Big Three would have made possible the inclusion of the amendment in the treaty. The Soviet Union, the Slav block, and some other states supported the Czechoslovak amendment.

In the early postwar period Prague believed that the expulsion of Hungarians would be a much simpler affair than that of the Germans. In August 1945, Under Secretary of State in the Foreign Ministry, Vladimir Clementis explained to the French Chargé d'Affaires, Keller, that the expulsion of Hungarians would not depend on the good will of the three Great Powers, but solely on approval of the Russian military authorities who alone were responsible for order in Hungary. Although Prague received Soviet diplomatic support for the expulsion of Hungarians, it appeared that this undertaking was not feasible solely on the basis of an agreement with Soviet officials. In view of the difficulties, Prague and Soviet diplomacy assumed and argued that the expulsion of the Germans from Hungary would facilitate the transfer of Hungarians from Slovakia to Hungary.

Atrocities committed during the German occupation in Hungary, created anti-German sentiment in the country and such feelings were expressed by leading politicians of the coalition parties. Several of their outstanding party members were arrested, tortured and executed by Arrow Cross authorities installed by the Nazis. Anti-German feelings were fostered by Soviet representatives in Budapest who pressed the Hungarian authorities to expel all Germans.

To increase pressure on the Hungarian government, at the Potsdam Conference the Soviets by a surprise move had proposed the transfer of the Germans from Hungary. Although the British and American delegations at Potsdam did not contemplate such action, they accepted the Soviet proposal. After this successful Soviet maneuver the tripartite agreement stated that "transfer to Germany of German populations, or elements thereof, remaining in Poland, Czechoslovakia and Hungary, will have to be undertaken. They agree, that any transfers that take place should be effected in an orderly and humane manner." Implications of the Potsdam decision became the major Czechoslovak and Soviet arguments at the Paris Conference. They claimed that the expulsion of all Germans from Hungary would make easy the transfer of Hungarians from Slovakia to Hungary.

As the peace conference progressed, we established good working relations with several delegations and asked for support in numerous instances and particularly in the case of the Czechoslovak amendments. The American delegation was understanding and American support was crucial but it was restricted. When Yugoslavia and Czechoslovakia proposed the transfer of materials from Hungarian archives and Envoy Gyula Szekfü asked Walter Bedell Smith, American representative in the Hungarian Commission, for support, Smith pointed out that it was more important to avoid human suffering with expulsion of Hungarians from Czechoslovakia than to block transfer of archival materials. It was clear that the United States delegation did not want to appear in the role of Hungary's protector against Allies, yet it was most important to obtain American support in the case of the Czechoslovak amendments.

The negative Soviet attitude toward Hungarian interests had indeed made clear before and during the conference that our diplomacy must look for Western support. Although events had shown that in the Soviet zone of Europe the Western powers had little influence and in some cases their diplomacy seemed uncertain if not counterproductive, Hungarian policy in the course of peace preparatory activities had continued to appeal to the West, in the face of Soviet opposition. Of course, we were aware of the new power situation along the Danube but it was a question of national honor to take a stand for our own sake, irrespective of outside support. As it turned out this attitude was no exercise in futility. Without strong United States opposition, 200,000 Hungarians would have been expelled from Czechoslovakia. In this case and in connection with a Czechoslovak claim to a piece of Hungarian territory opposite Bratislava across the Danube, we had close contacts with the American delegation. John C. Campbell, a member of the American delegation, characterized this relationship:

> On these questions, with my colleagues Philip Mosely and Fred Merrill, I was in close contact with Stephen Kertesz and with Aladar Szegedy-Maszak, the Hungarian Minister to the United States. We consulted. They asked our advice about their delegation's draft statements, about what they should say that might have a chance of getting support and acceptance by the United States, what might be the best strategy at the conference meetings in dealing with what the Russians and the Czechs might do, and so on. There was perhaps, something incongruous in this business of representatives of a defeated enemy state and of a victorious allied state getting together to concert a strategy against other victorious allied states, but that's the way it was . . .
>
> And it was right, I thought at the time and I still think now, for the United States to support the Hungarian position on those issues. We were trying to save whatever chance there might be for the democratic elements in Hungary to prevail or at least to survive in their country, and there were questions of principle involved in the

question of the expulsion of Hungarians from Czechoslovakia. We stood, as Hungary stood, for the principle that there is no collective guilt, and no collective punishment, for those of a particular ethnic group for whatever reason. It was a principle, incidentally, which we had already violated at the Potsdam conference with respect to Germans from eastern Europe, but that was no reason why we should violate it again.

American opposition to expulsion of Hungarians from Czechoslovakia was all-important. But at the same time we had to obtain the support of as many countries as possible, large or small, because Secretary Byrnes pledged the United States would automatically accept any decision voted by two-third majority in the plenary session of the conference and Czechoslovakia had many friends among the victorious states.

During the critical period of negotiations I was involved in several semi-official conversations that threw light on the way of thinking of some delegations. General Pope, representative of the Canadian delegation in the Hungarian Subcommittee, invited me to luncheon in his Hotel Crillon apartment on September 15, and during our long conversation tried to persuade me of the necessity of compromise in connection with transfer of Hungarians from Czechoslovakia. I explained to him the reasons of our opposition.

Lord Hood invited me to visit him at the headquarters of the British delegation. He was interested in my evaluation concerning the probable votes of various delegations with respect to the Czechoslovak amendment, and I shared with him all information we had. Then he asked me what the Hungarian delegation would do if the conference accepted the amendment. I told him that the Hungarian government would send new instructions and added that personally I would buy a railroad ticket to Budapest because I did not see any reason why the Hungarian delegation should remain in Paris after such a catastrophic decision. I pointed out that the coalition government surely would collapse. A few days later Hood opposed the imposition of unilateral solutions concerning the Hungarian minorities in Czechoslovakia. After some hesitation, Britain and Canada finally decided to follow the United States in opposing the Czechoslovak amendment.

Costello, a delegate of New Zealand, rapporteur of the Hungarian

Subcommittee, came to see me unexpectedly in the Claridge on September 29 and informed me during luncheon that his government had instructed his delegation to support the Czechoslovak amendment for expulsion of Hungarians. He pointed out that the United States, Britain, Australia and the Union of South Africa were against the amendment, but that the five Slav states together with France and New Zealand would vote for it. With possible support of India, Canada, and some other states, the amendment might obtain the two-third majority that would change the position of the United States. In view of this possibility he recommended a compromise, the transfer of Hungarians in ten years, with a yearly quota of 20,000. He expressed fear that in the case of our refusal the Hungarian population of Slovakia would be transferred to remote parts of the USSR. I refused to entertain this possibility and told him we were not willing to accept the transfer of Hungarians from Czechoslovakia under any conditions, in any shape or form. Costello became strikingly depressed during our conversation and concluded that he was "frightfully sorry" because of the negative result of our exchange of views.

Although the Yugoslavs supported the Czechoslovak amendments, their attitude was more moderate than that of the Soviets. Yet the secretary general of the Yugoslav delegation. Jŏze Vilfan, asked me on August 17 to meet him urgently. When we met, he informed me that unless the Hungarian delegation was willing to sign an agreement on hydrographic questions and another on minority population exchange, the Yugoslav government would request the conference to insert such amendments in the peace treaty. Since the deadline for amendments was August 19, he indicated that the bilateral treaties must be signed within forty-eight hours. I told Vilfan that both treaties would involve negotiations about highly technical questions and so it was impossible to complete, let alone sign, such agreements within a couple of days. During these days our efforts had been concentrated to defeat the Czechoslovak amendments and the purpose of the Yugoslav action might have been to put additional pressure on us. The chairmen of the Hungarian and Yugoslav delegations agreed later that on the basis of a *voluntary* exchange of minority population, Hungary and Yugoslavia would exchange a maximum of 40,000 inhabitants of each country. The Yugoslav amendment was withdrawn and the exchange agreement was not implemented.

The peace treaty instead of the Czechoslovak amendment obligated Hungary to enter negotiations with Czechoslovakia to solve the problem of the latter's inhabitants of Hungarian ethnic origin. This incident at the Paris Conference was one of the consequences of the Czechoslovak policy initiated in 1945 to expel all non-Slavic inhabitants. In the spirit of Hitlerite legislation, Hungarians were deprived of their citizenship, of all political rights, and elementary human rights, and they were persecuted by a series of administrative measures. The Hungarian government was forced to conclude a population exchange agreement with Czechoslovakia in February 1946. Through this exchange, expulsions and because of persecution over 90,000 Hungarians left Czechoslovakia for Hungary, that is about twelve percent of the Hungarian population of Slovakia.

The other Czechoslovak amendment, which demanded transfer of five Hungarian villages for enlargement of the Bratislava bridgehead on the right bank of the Danube, ended with a compromise. Although it was difficult to find compelling reasons for this Czechoslovak proposal, except expansion for expansions sake, the peace treaty transferred three villages to Czechoslovakia: Horvatjárfalu, Oroszvár, Dunacsún. The conference would not approve the Czechoslovak amendment for expulsion of 200,000 Hungarians, and the Allied powers, in a spirit of diplomatic compromise, apparently wanted to give some satisfaction to Prague.

Peacemaking in 1945–47 was not much more than recasting the armistice agreements with some trimming into peace treaties and this meant the implicit recognition of an unprecedented division of the Old Continent, coupled with the erection of an iron curtain which still exists throughout Central Europe. After the ratification of the peace treaties, unlimited Soviet troops remained in Hungary and Rumania to maintain the lines of communication with the Soviet zone in Austria. Wartime and postwar policy was influenced by geography and by the fact that Britain and the United States did not have major economic or other interests in any East European or Danubian country. Whatever the explanation, the new status quo in Europe greatly reduced the rimland necessary for defense of the Western world and shifted one hundred million people into the zone of Soviet domination.

List of
Documents

List of Documents

PLANNING FOR PEACE IN THE FOG OF WAR

1. The Four Freedoms (January 6, 1941)
2. Atlantic Charter (August 14, 1941)
3. Unconditional Surrender (January 24, 1943)
4. United States Interests and Policy in Eastern and South-eastern Europe and the Near East. Memorandum by the Undersecretary of State (Stettinius) to President Roosevelt (November 8, 1944)
5. Briefing Book Paper Prepared for the Yalta Conference on "Principal Hungarian Problems"
6. The Yalta Declaration on Liberated Europe (February 11, 1945)

POSTWAR PATTERNS OF PEACEMAKING

7. "General Approach to the Peace Treaties with Rumania, Bulgaria and Hungary." (This undated State Department document was apparently written immediately after the Potsdam Conference)
8. Memorandum of the visit of H. Freeman Matthews (head of the European Division in the State Department) in the French Foreign Ministry on December 31, 1945. He transmitted to Jean Chauvel (Secretary General of the French Foreign Ministry) Secretary James F. Byrnes' message concerning the result of the Moscow Conference.
9. Ambassador Dejean's Report from Prague to Paris concerning Czechoslovak Reaction to France's exclusion from the Moscow Conference (January 3, 1946)
10. Secretary of State James F. Byrnes' Statement concerning France's Participation in the Council of Foreign Ministers and the Peace Conference (January 13, 1946)

EX-ENEMY STATES AT THE PEACE TABLE

Hungarian Peace Preparatory Notes and Ambassador W. Averell Harriman's and Minister H. F. Arthur Schoenfeld's Reports to Washington

THE TRANSYLVANIAN QUESTION AND THE HUNGARIAN GOVERNMENT DELEGATION'S VISIT TO MOSCOW (APRIL 9 TO APRIL 18, 1946)

HUNGARO-CZECHOSLOVAK CONFLICT AND THE PARIS CONFERENCE

Hungarian Ministry for Foreign Affairs in 1947 on *Hungary and the Conference of Paris*

30. Stephen Kertesz, "The Expulsion of the Germans from Hungary: A Study in Postwar Diplomacy," *The Review of Politics,* Vol. 15, (1953), 179–208

I.

Planning for Peace in the Fog of War: Wartime Statements and Documents

THE FOUR FREEDOMS DOCUMENT NO. 1

Annual Message of the President to the Congress, January 6, 1941 (Excerpt)*

In the future days, which we seek to make secure, we look forward to a world founded upon four essential human freedoms.

The first is freedom of speech and expression—everywhere in the world.

The second is freedom of every person to worship God in his way—everywhere in the world.

The third is freedom from want—which, translated into world terms, means economic understandings which will secure to every nation a healthy peacetime life for its inhabitants—everywhere in the world.

The fourth is freedom from fear—which, translated into world terms, means a world-wide reduction of armaments to such a point and in such a thorough fashion that no nation will be in a position to commit an act of physical aggression against any neighbor—anywhere in the world.

*Development of United States Foreign Policy, S. Doc. 188, 77th Cong., 2d sess., pp. 86–87.

ATLANTIC CHARTER DOCUMENT NO. 2

Declaration by the President of the United States and the Prime Minister of the United Kingdom, August 14, 1941*

[Four months before Pearl Harbor, President Roosevelt and Prime Minister Churchill met on the high seas and drew up the Atlantic Charter. The Charter not only provided an important statement of war aims for World War II; it also notified the world that increasing coöperation between the two great English-speaking countries might be expected in the face of a common danger. At the time, there was much comment about the exact meaning of the Charter and the binding nature of the commitments assumed by the two governments. It was not drawn up as a formal international agreement.]

Joint declaration of the President of the United States of America and the Prime Minister, Mr. Churchill, representing His Majesty's Government in the United Kingdom, being met together, deem it right to make known certain common principles in the national policies of their respective countries on which they base their hopes for a better future for the world.

First, their countries seek no aggrandizement, territorial or other;

Second, they desire to see no territorial changes that do not accord with the freely expressed wishes of the peoples concerned;

Third, they respect the right of all peoples to choose the form of government under which they will live; and they wish to see sovereign rights and self-government restored to those who have been forcibly deprived of them;

Fourth, they will endeavor, with due respect for their existing obligations, to further the enjoyment by all States, great or small,

---

*Cooperative War Effort, Department of State publication 1732, Executive Agreement Series 236, p. 4.

victor or vanquished, of access, on equal terms, to the trade and to the raw materials of the world which are needed for their economic prosperity;

Fifth, they desire to bring about the fullest collaboration between all nations in the economic field with the object of securing, for all, improved labor standards, economic advancement and social security;

Sixth, after the final destruction of the Nazi tyranny, they hope to see established a peace which will afford to all nations the means of dwelling in safety within their own boundaries, and which will afford assurance that all the men in all the lands may live out their lives in freedom from fear and want;

Seventh, such a peace should enable all men to traverse the high seas and oceans without hindrance;

Eighth, they believe that all of the nations of the world, for realistic as well as spiritual reasons must come to the abandonment of the use of force. Since no future peace can be maintained if land, sea or air armaments continue to be employed by nations which threaten, or may threaten, aggression outside of their frontiers, they believe, pending the establishment of a wider and permanent system of general security, that the disarmament of such nations is essential. They will likewise aid and encourage all other practicable measures which will lighten for peace-loving peoples the crushing burden of armaments.

"UNCONDITIONAL SURRENDER"*

DOCUMENT NO. 3

On January 24, 1943, during the Roosevelt-Churchill conference at Casablanca, the President announced the doctrine of unconditional surrender—that the Allies would accept nothing less than the unconditional surrender of their foes.

> ...The President and the Prime Minister, after a complete survey of the world war situation, are more than ever determined that peace can come to the world only by a total elimination of German and Japanese war power. This involves the simple formula of placing the objective of this war in terms of an unconditional surrender by Germany, Italy and Japan. Unconditional surrender by them means a reasonable assurance of world peace, for generations. Unconditional surrender means not the destruction of the German populace, nor of the Italian or Japanese populace, but does mean the destruction of a philosophy in Germany, Italy and Japan which is based on the conquest and subjugation of other peoples.
>
> The President and the Prime Minister are confident that this is equally the purpose of Russia, of China, and of all other members of the United Nations. ...

---

*Notes by FDR, Jan. 22-23, 1943, *Foreign Relations of the United States: The Conferences at Washington, 1941-1942, and Casablanca, 1943* (Washington, D.C.: Government Printing Office, 1968), p. 837.

DOCUMENT NO. 4
Memorandum by the Under Secretary of State (Stettinius) to President Roosevelt

WASHINGTON, November 8, 1944.

United States Interests and Policy in Eastern and Southeastern Europe and the Near East*

While the Government of the United States is fully aware of the existence of problems between Great Britain and the Soviet Union, this Government should not assume the attitude of supporting either country as against the other. Rather, this Government should assert the independent interest of the United States (which is also believed to be in the general interest) in favor of equitable arrangements designed to attain general peace and security on a basis of good neighborship, and should not assume that the American interest requires it at this time to identify its interests with those of either the Soviet Union or Great Britain.

In Eastern and Southeastern Europe and the Near East, as elsewhere, the United States Government should consistently maintain and actively endeavor to further the following general principles irrespective of the type of territorial or political settlements which may result from the war:

1. The right of peoples to choose and maintain for themselves without outside interference the type of political, social, and economic systems they desire, so long as they conduct their affairs in such a way as not to menace the peace and security of others.

2. Equality of opportunity, as against the setting up of a policy of exclusion, in commerce, transit and trade; and freedom to negotiate, either through government agencies or private enterprise, irrespective of the type of economic system in operation.

---

*Foreign Relations of the United States (hereafter FRUS), 1944, 4, pp. 1025–26.

57

3. The right of access to all countries on an equal and unrestricted basis of bona fide representatives of the recognized press, radio, newsreel and information agencies of other nations engaged in gathering news and other forms of public information for dissemination to the public in their own countries; and the right to transmit information gathered by them to points outside such territories without hindrance or discrimination.

4. Freedom for American philanthropic and educational organizations to carry on their activities in the respective countries on the basis of most-favored-nation treatment.

5. General protection of American citizens and the protection and furtherance of legitimate American economic rights, existing or potential.

6. The United States maintains the general position that territorial settlements should be left until the end of the war.

Briefing Book Paper DOCUMENT NO. 5

PRINCIPAL HUNGARIAN PROBLEMS*

Summary

The long-range interest of the United States in the maintenance of peace and stability in central Europe may be involved in the issues now arising in connection with terms of armistice for Hungary, with the control of Hungary during the armistice period, and with the territorial settlement. The two most pressing problems are (1) the share which the United States will have in the work of the Allied Control Commission, and (2) the payment of reparation by Hungary.

It is possible that Soviet and American policy may not be in harmony if the Soviet Union uses its position as the power in actual control of the execution of the armistice to intervene in Hungarian domestic affairs, to dominate Hungary, or to pursue a severe policy on the reparation question which would cripple Hungarian economy and thus delay the economic recovery of Europe and the restoration of normal economic relationships based on equal treatment for all nations.

While American and British interests are more or less the same in these questions, we prefer an independent approach to the Russians and should seek agreement on solutions and procedures which take account of the interests of all these and of the other United Nations. It would be desirable to secure the agreement of the British and Soviet Governments to the following principles:

1. Participation of the American and British Governments in the execution of the armistice to the maximum degree consistent with leaving to the Soviet High Command decisions connected with the conduct of military operations; after Germany's surrender

---

*FRUS, 1945. "The Conference of Malta and Yalta," pp. 242–45.

all three Governments should have equal representation and responsibility;

2. An Allied economic policy toward Hungary which will reconcile legitimate claims of Allied nations to reparation with the general interest in promoting the rapid economic recovery of Europe;

3. The desirability of reaching a settlement of the Hungarian-Rumanian frontier dispute and of encouraging an eventual settlement between Hungary and Czechoslovakia and perhaps between Hungary and Yugoslavia, by friendly mutual negotiation, which would take into account the Hungarian ethnic claims.

PRINCIPAL HUNGARIAN PROBLEMS

Long-Range American Interest in Hungary

The long-range interest of the United States in Hungary centers in our desire to see established peaceful and stable relationships among European nations. The United States has an interest in the achievement of solutions of Hungary's boundary disputes and its political and economic problems which will promote orderly progress and peace with neighboring states. We believe this interest would be served by a territorial settlement which would rectify the frontier with Rumania in favor of Hungary on ethnic grounds. While Hungary must of course renounce the territorial gains made at the expense of Czechoslovakia and Yugoslavia with German help, the United States would favor, for example, an eventual negotiated settlement which would transfer to Hungary some of the predominantly Hungarian-populated districts of southern Slovakia. Economically, the United States has an interest in maintaining equal treatment and opportunity in Hungary for all nations. The largest single private American interest in Hungary is the petroleum company "Maort", owned by the Standard Oil Company of New Jersey; the fields in its concession have excellent prospects for future development.

At present Hungary, as an enemy state which has been associated with Germany's aggressions since 1938 and the last satellite to desert the Axis, has no valid claim to leniency on the part of the Allies. During the period of the armistice Hungary must be subjected to Allied control and must be required to make some reparation for war damages. It is not in the interest of the United States, however, to see Hungary deprived of its independence or of any of its pre-1938 territories or saddled with economic obligations which would cripple its economy and thus delay general European economic recovery.

American Policy on Immediate Questions concerning Hungary

The "Provisional National Government of Hungary" formed on December 23, 1944, at Debrecen in the Soviet-occupied portion of Hungary, has asked the Allies for an armistice and has declared war on Germany. This body appears to represent the significant pro-Allied political forces in Hungary today. While the United States has not yet recognized it as a provisional government, it is probable that it will be so recognized and that the armistice terms, upon which the three principal Allies are now reaching agreement, will be presented to it.

The United States has agreed that the general pattern of the Rumanian armistice terms should be applied in the case of Hungary, with two important exceptions:

1. In the matter of the Allied Control Commission for Hungary, this Government is attempting to secure Soviet agreement to a clear definition of the rights and powers which the American representatives on the Commission will have. Lack of such an understanding at the start in the cases of Rumania and Bulgaria has made the position of our representatives on the Control Commissions for those two countries difficult. This Government desires to avoid a state of affairs whereby it becomes a signatory to the armistice and by accepting representation on an "Allied" Control Commission assumes some responsibility for its execution, but is in fact without influence and may not even be consulted on the decisions taken by the Soviet authorities acting in the name of the Allied Control Commission. We believe that, at the very least, our representatives should be consulted on such decisions. The United States has proposed also that after the termination of hostilities

against Germany the three principal Allies should have equal participation in the operation of the Control Commission.

2. The second important point is the reparation settlement with Hungary. In the negotiations on armistice terms, the United States Government is attempting, so far without success, to secure Soviet agreement to American and British participation, through membership on a reparation section of the Control Commission, in the actual working out and supervision of the reparation deliveries and payments by Hungary to members of the United Nations.

Consideration is being given to the advisability of standing firm on the questions of the Control Commission and of reparation to the point of signing the armistice with a formal reservation on one or both of them.

American Policy in the Armistice Period

While the United States would not, of course, take the position of supporting Hungary against the Soviet Union, it is possible that American and Soviet policies toward Hungary during the armistice period may not be in harmony, especially if there is an absence of agreement on some of the important armistice terms or if the position gained by the Soviet Union by virtue of its military campaign and under the armistice agreement is used to dominate Hungary or to strip it of a great part of its resources.

The United States Government recognizes that the Soviet Union's interest in Hungary is more direct than ours. We have had no objection to the Soviet Government's taking the lead in the negotiations for the armistice and in the control of Hungary in the armistice period until the surrender of Germany. We do not, however, consider that the Soviet Union has any special privileged or dominant position in Hungary. In the armistice period we expect to have a civilian mission in Hungary headed by Mr. H. F. Arthur Schoenfeld, who will have the personal rank of Minister and will maintain informal relations with the Hungarian Government. Soviet agreement to this representation seems assured.

The interests of the United States would be served by the conclusion of peace with Hungary at the earliest practicable date. Such a step would put an end to many of the powers of control which under the armistice will be exercised by the Soviet Union, and by opening the way to the resumption of normal diplomatic relations between the United States and Hungary would give the United States Government a better opportunity to protect American interests in that country.

It is also in our interest that free elections be held and that Hungary be left to manage its own internal affairs as soon as possible.

DECLARATION ON LIBERATED EUROPE*

DOCUMENT NO. 6

We have drawn up and subscribed to a Declaration on Liberated Europe. This Declaration provides for concerting the policies of the three Powers and for joint action by them in meeting the political and economic problems of liberated Europe in accordance with democratic principles. The text of the Declaration is as follows:

> The Premier of the Union of Soviet Socialist Republics, the Prime Minister of the United Kingdom, and the President of the United States of America have consulted with each other in the common interests of the peoples of their countries and those of liberated Europe. They jointly declare their mutual agreement to concert during the temporary period of instability in liberated Europe the policies of their three governments in assisting the peoples liberated from the domination of Nazi Germany and the peoples of the former Axis satellite states of Europe to solve by democratic means their pressing political and economic problems.
>
> The establishment of order in Europe and the rebuilding of national economic life must be achieved by processes which will enable the liberated peoples to destroy the last vestiges of Nazism and Fascism and to creat[e] democratic institutions of their own choice. This is a principle of the Atlantic Charter—the right of all peoples to choose the form of government under which they will live—the restoration of sovereign rights and self-government to those peoples who have been forcibly deprived of them by the aggressor nations.

---

*FRUS, 1945, "The Conference of Malta and Yalta," pp. 971-73.

To foster the conditions in which the liberated peoples may exercise these rights, the three governments will jointly assist the people in any European liberated state or former Axis satellite state in Europe where in their judgment conditions require (a) to establish conditions of internal peace; (b) to carry out emergency measures for the relief of distressed people; (c) to form interim governmental authorities broadly representative of all democratic elements in the population and pledged to the earliest possible establishment through free elections of governments responsive to the will of the people; and (d) to facilitate where necessary the holding of such elections.

The three governments will consult the other United Nations and provisional authorities or other governments in Europe when matters of direct interest to them are under consideration.

When, in the opinion of the three governments, conditions in any European liberated state or any former Axis satellite state in Europe make such action necessary, they will immediately consult together on the measures necessary to discharge the joint responsibilities set forth in this declaration.

By this declaration we reaffirm our faith in the principles of the Atlantic Charter, our pledge in the Declaration by the United Nations, and our determination to build in cooperation with other peace-loving nations a world order under law, dedicated to peace, security, freedom and the general well-being of all mankind.

In issuing this declaration, the Three Powers express the hope that the Provisional Government of the French Republic may be associated with them in the procedure suggested.

II

Postwar Patterns of Peacemaking: Diplomatic Problems at the Potsdam and Moscow Conferences and the Issue of France's Exclusion

DOCUMENT NO. 7
General Approach to the Peace Treaties with Rumania, Bulgaria and Hungary*

From the time of the declarations of war by the three Axis satellites on the United States in December 1941 this Government has taken the view that the peoples of these enemy states were forced into the war on Germany's side against their will. President Roosevelt, in recommending that the Congress recognise a state of war between the United States and Rumania, Bulgaria and Hungary (June 1942), said: "I realize that the three Governments took this action not upon their own initiative or in response to the wishes of their own peoples but as the instruments of Hitler".

The American attitude toward the Axis satellites has differed sharply from our attitude toward Germany. This fact is evident from the wording of the appeals addressed to the former to break with Germany and get out of the war. When they did surrender they were granted armistice terms which did not represent unconditional surrender. They subsequently declared war on Germany, and Rumania and Bulgaria made definite military contributions in the campaigns on the eastern front.

In the Crimea Declaration on Liberated Europe (February 11, 1945) the three principal Allies put the former Axis satellites on the same plane with the liberated states in agreeing to provide assistance in solving pressing political and economic problems arising from the war. At Potsdam (August 2, 1945) it was agreed that the three principal Allies should examine the reestablishment of diplomatic relations with the ex-satellites and prepare peace treaties for them, following the signature of which applications by

---

*Box 97, RG-43, National Archives (hereafter N.A.)

them for membership in the United Nations Organization would be supported.

In accordance with this general attitude toward the three ex-satellites, it is the view of the Department of State that the peace treaties with them should not be of a punitive character. "War guilt" clauses, unjustified territorial amputations, and undue military, political or economic restrictions would not be included in the treaties. It is hoped by this policy to avoid the division of the Central European and Balkan region into irreconcilable groups of "status quo" and "revisionist" states, which was one of the consequences of the last peace settlement and was one reason why Southeastern Europe fell so easily under German domination. In the interest of a durable settlement it is desired to conclude peace treaties which will make possible the early entry of the three ex-enemy states into the United Nations Organization and the establishment of mutual friendly relations among all the nations of this region.

It is believed that general security in the Danubian-Balkan area can be better secured by the United Nations Organization and by regional arrangements which are in conformity with the United Nations Charter than by specific treaty restrictions on the military establishments or on the industries of the ex-satellite states. Similarly, it would be undesirable to impose heavy economic burdens on these states which would make the general economic recovery of Europe more difficult and would probably in the end be more costly to the United States.

While the peace terms should not be "harsh", they should nevertheless not be such as to give the impression that these ex-enemy nations are being rewarded for their decision to fight on the side of the Axis or are being favored over nations which resisted Germany and fought on the side of the United Nations.

DOCUMENT NO. 8
DIRECTION POLITIQUE*

Paris, le 31 Décembre 1945.

M. Matthews, Directeur d'Europe au Département d'Etat à Washington, de passage à Paris à son retour de Moscou, est venu voir M. Chauvel pour faire une communication de la part de M. Byrnes. Il s'agissait de donner au Gouvernement français l'assurance:

1° que le Gouvernement des Etats-Unis attachait une grande importance à l'adhésion de la France au plan proposé pour la préparation des Traités de Paix;

2° qu'aucune question intéressant directement la France n'avait été discutée à Moscou et que le communiqué publié mentionnait tous les accords auxquels les trois Ministres étaient arrivés.

M. Matthews a ajouté qu'un certain nombre de questions autres que celles figurant sur le communiqué avaient été discutées, mais sans qu'aucun accord put être établi.

Il s'agit en premier lieu du problème de l'Iran. La délégation anglaise a présenté un projet transactionnel au sujet du régime de l'Azerbeidjan, mais la délégation soviétique a refusé de discuter ce projet.

La situation de la Turquie a été examinée également sans autre résultat que des déclarations du côté soviétique disant que l'U.R.S.S. n'avait aucune intention agressive vis-à-vis de ce pays.

En ce qui concerne l'Allemagne, trois problèmes relativement secondaires ont été abordés, à savoir:

1) le maintien dans la zone britannique d'importantes formations militaires allemandes, question qui a été réglée entre temps au Comité de Contrôle de Berlin;

2) le rapatriement des ressortissants des pays annexés par l'U.R.S.S., question déjà discutée sans résultat à la Conférence de Londres;

3) le partage de la flotte de pêche allemande. Sur ce point la délégation russe demandait une décision immédiate. Les délégations

---

*Série Y, Carton 45, Dossier 7, Archives du ministère des Affaires étrangères (hereafter MAE).

américaine et britannique ont refusé, en demandant le renvoi au Comité de Contrôle de Berlin.

M. Matthews a été informé du sens dans lequel serait sans doute rédigée la réponse française à l'invitation d'adhérer à une nouvelle procédure pour l'établissement des traités de Paix.

Il n'a pas dissimulé que les difficultés avaient été grandes à Moscou pour arriver à la solution transactionnelle proposée. Les Russes en effet se refusaient à accepter une Conférence de Paix et s'en tenaient à l'idée que les traités devaient être établis par les seuls trois Grands. La solution proposée maintenant est un compromis très laborieusement établi.

M. Matthews a ajouté que si le Gouvernement français demandait des éclaircissements, la réponse devrait naturellement être concertée entre les trois Gouvernements et que ceci ne serait pas aisé.

A une question posée sur le sort désormais réservé à la Conférence des Ministres des Affaires Etrangères, il a répondu que rien n'avait été modifié du mécanisme prévu à Potsdam et que d'ailleurs c'étaient les représentants désignés des Ministres qui devaient se réunir prochainement à Londres.

M. Matthews a dit aussi que la Conférence de la Paix n'était pas une création spectaculaire et qu'elle aurait une autorité réelle./.

DOCUMENT NO. 9
AFFAIRES ÉTRANGÈRES TÉLÉGRAMME A L'ARRIVÉE*

SECRET

PRAGUE, le 3 Janvier 1946 à 21 h.15
reçu le 4 Janvier à 15 H.30
n° 11 à 13

RESERVE –
URGENT

Lors de la (présentation) des voeux au Président de la République, j'avais perçu dans les quelques mots échangés avec M. BENES combien celui-ci était affecté des décisions prises à Moscou à l'égard de la France.

M. MASARYK, avec lequel je me suis entretenu ce matin, 3 Janvier, à la veille de son départ pour (Londres) m'a dit que l'élimination de notre pays du règlement général de la paix était pour la Tchécoslovaquie "un véritable désastre."

Les Britanniques, m'a-t-il dit, n'étaient guère en mesure de vous soutenir mais comment BYRNES n'a-t-il pas compris qu'en barrant la France, il abandonnait toute l'Europe à une seule puissance ? Une telle hégémonie n'est donc l'intérêt de personne pas même de la Russie soviétique (.)

D'après les rapports parvenus au Palais CZERNIN sur (les) réceptions auxquelles la Conférence a donné lieu au Kremlin, M. MOLOTOFF a affecté à l'égard de M. BYRNES la plus grande cordialité. En revanche (il a) ostensiblement négligé M. BEVIN comme pour bien marquer au Secrétaire d'Etat Britannique qu'il n'était que toléré dans la Compagnie (des) 3 Grands.

---

*MAE, Série Y, Carton 45, Dossier 7.

A bien des égards, la Conférence de Moscou évoquait l'entrevue de Tilsitt plutôt que les réunions dans le style de Yalta.

J'adresse au Département sous (forme) (de) télégramme en clair par courrier un compte-rendu plus détaillé de l'impression produite ici par la Conférence de Moscou./.

DEJEAN

(
DIFFUSION) Général de GAULLE
(CABINET
) M. CHAUVEL

DOCUMENT NO. 10

Text of a note delivered to the French Government by the Secretary of State Byrnes, on January 13. It was being released simultaneously in London, Paris, and Washington.*

I am happy to note that the French Government has expressed its willingness to take part in the proposed Conference for the consideration of peace treaties and is ready so far as it is concerned to invite all the Governments envisaged in the proposal to send their representatives to the Conference at Paris.

In order that the French Government may be in a position to confirm this understanding, I am glad to furnish in response to the French Government's request for clarification, the following explanations and information in the name of the Governments of the United States of America, the Union of Soviet Socialist Republics and the United Kingdom:

1 — The French Government desires to be informed of the future work of the Council of the Foreign Ministers. It is our understanding that the future role of the Council of Foreign Ministers is that provided in the Potsdam Agreement with the exception that after the Peace Conference is held the states which are signatory to the Armistice will draft the final treaty, taking into account the recommendations of the Peace Conference. As stated in the French Government's communication, the Potsdam Agreement provided for the preparation of the peace settlement with Germany. The agreement reached at Moscow is in no way intended to alter the previous understanding with regard to the preparation of the peace settlement with Germany. Furthermore, the Potsdam Agreement likewise provided that other work might be assigned to the Council from time to time by the member

*The Department of State Bulletin, 12 (1946), 112-13.

Governments. No change in this provision was anticipated at Moscow.

2—In response to point 2 of the French communication it may be stated that the Potsdam Agreement provided for the possibility that the Council of Foreign Ministers might invite the representatives of other Governments when matters which particularly concerned them were to be discussed. Inasmuch as the Moscow agreement did not seek to repeal the Potsdam Agreement, the Council retains the authority to invite any state to participate in the discussions whenever there is pending a matter of direct interest to such state. The Council, as constituted for the preparation of specific treaties, or the Deputies of the Powers represented for that purpose may determine from time to time, when such matters arise and are authorized to extend invitations.

3—The French Government may rest assured that as broad and thorough a discussion as possible shall take place at the forthcoming Conference and that the final drafts of the treaties will be made only after the fullest consideration has been given to the recommendations of the Conference. We have no doubt that no final treaty would be concluded which arbitrarily rejected the recommendations of the Conference.

4—With respect to the views of the states with which the treaties are to be concluded, the work of preparation for the draft treaties will take into account the views of these states and adequate opportunities will be given these states to discuss the treaties and to present their views both in the formulation of the drafts as was permitted in the earlier meetings in London, and at the May Conference. It is agreed that this does not constitute a precedent for peace settlements which are not the subject of the present discussions.

It is believed that the foregoing explanation will provide the information necessary for the determination of the functions of the proposed Conference, and it is hoped that the French Government will now be in a position to confirm its agreement to participate in the proposed Conference.

III

Ex-Enemy States at the Peace Table

A.
Hungarian Peace Preparatory Notes and Ambassador W. Averell Harriman's and Minister H. F. Arthur Schoenfeld's Reports to Washington

DOCUMENT NO. 11

Hungarian Ministry for Foreign Affairs.

Budapest, August 14th. 1945.

44 (res) Be.

1945.

Sir,

The democratic Hungarian Government wishes to express its deep gratitude to His Britannic Majesty's Government for the good will they have displayed towards Hungary during the Potsdam Conference when our country's fate was being discussed.

The Hungarian Government is especially grateful for that part of the communiqué issued at the close of the conference which makes it possible for Hungary to conclude a peace treaty in the near future, foreshadowing, as it does, our eventual admission into the organisation of the United Nations. This will enable the Hungarian people to join the community of democratic states. Hungary wishes to participate actively and without reservation in the work of the new world organisation which is predestined to lead the nations towards a happier future.

At the time of the forthcoming peace negotiations the Hungarian Government does not desire to stress particular Hungarian interests.

It is our wish that the peace treaties to be concluded should adjust the Hungarian problems with due consideration for the cause of world peace, bearing in mind the special interests of the Central European community. Hungarian interests will also best be served by a peace which brings tranquillity to the peoples ravaged by the war and which achieves satisfaction to the widest possible extent facilitating peaceful co-operation with foreign states, especially our neighbours.

Starting from this guiding principle the Hungarian Government recommends that the following general considerations should form the basis of the peace negotiations adjusting the political, territorial, cultural and economic problems:

1. The preliminary requirements of the welfare of the small nations living in the Danube valley is that their close economic co-operation should be realised. It is a well-known fact that the cost of agricultural production in these countries is much higher — for reasons which cannot be enumerated here but which were thoroughly investigated by the Hungarian Government — than in the large wheat-growing countries which establish world prices. Similarly the production cost of most of the manufactured goods in South-eastern Europe is higher than world prices. The nations of this region are so interdependent economically that they must be either enemies or friends.

Under these circumstances the prosperity of the peoples of South-Eastern Europe can only be put on a solid basis if their close economic co-operation and reciprocal trade is institutionally secured.

The Austro-Hungarian Monarchy was undoubtedly obsolete politically, but it was better equipped on account of its widespread borders extending from Passau to Pola and Predeal to assure the welfare of its peoples than the small succession states carved out of it. The latter being impelled by excessive chauvinism tried to achieve unsound autarchy and adopted an economic policy of mutual exclusion which proved to be extremely detrimental to the welfare of their peoples. . . .

This unsound and irrational economic policy paved the way for the German economic penetration which none of the states were able to withstand, especially during the recurring economic crises.

Therefore the peace treaties should strive to ensure institutionally that the small Danubian nations, complementary to one another in natural resources and economically dependent upon each other, pursue the policy of closest economic co-operation instead of economic isolation. This would materially minimize the political controversies and dissensions and at the same time benefit world economy. The economic advancement of the Danubian countries would also augment their importance as consumer markets.

Here it is necessary to point out that in the commercial agreement between the United States of America and Czechoslovakia in 1935, the United States agreed not to claim under the most favoured nation clause any benefits that Czechoslovakia would confer on Austria, Roumania, Hungary or Yougoslavia. Thus the Government of the United States acknowledged at that time the special relationship existing between the Danubian States.

In view of the aforesaid the Hungarian Government on its part deems it desirable that the Powers responsible for the territorial reconstruction of the Danubian region state their views as to how the effective economic co-operation of the Danubian states can be institutionally secured.

2. In this connection the Hungarian Government requests that when the reconstruction of the Danubian region is undertaken the increased industrialization of Hungary should be made feasible.

Here is indeed the crux of the situation: Hungary as an agrarian state can only take care of the increase in her population through the thorough reorganization of her economic system. There is no doubt that the reorganization of her agricultural production will necessitate large-scale capital investment, considerable time and favourable economic conditions. But even with the reorganization of agriculture the greater part of the natural increase in population will still have to seek employment in other industries.

Between 1900 and 1941 the population of present-day Hungary increased by 2,463,000; out of this only 373,000 could find employment in agriculture. Other industries, mainly manufacturing, had to absorb the rest, about 2,090,000.

The natural growth of agrarian population during the last four decades, about one and a half million people, was lost for agriculture. This serves as irrefutable proof for the need of industrialization. . . .

The industrialization of South-Eastern Europe could be made easier if some of the German industries to be discontinued were reassembled in this region. In this event the economic dependency of these countries on Germany would cease to a large extent, and German expansion to the East would be drastically checked. Formerly the German industrial expansion has been towards the East, so its resettlement here would continue the natural trend.

When advocating this plan the Hungarian Government does not wish to advocate economic self-sufficiency. This would not be in accord with our previous remarks about the necessity of economic collaboration between the Danubian countries. Every South-Eastern European country should be given an opportunity to develop those industries which complement its natural resources. In Hungary for instance it would mean the establishment of industries connected with agriculture and fruit growing, as well as of those industries which have the requisite raw materials for developed production (for instance bauxite, oil, natural gas) and the reconstruction and improvement of existing industries such as chemical industries, manufacturing chemists, etc.

3. Economic co-operation however has certain ideological prerequisites. In other words public opinion in the South-eastern European countries must be trained in the art of good neighbourliness instead of enmity as in the past. The last traces of racial theory created by German chauvinism must be eradicated to prevent the recurrence of the evil effects of racial intolerance throughout the world. One of the most important tasks of all nations should be the total elimination of all Nazi doctrines from their ideologies.

Therefore in the opinion of the Hungarian Government it is essential that public education should be basically changed from that existing between the two world wars, as well as the press and all political publications in the Danubian countries, all of them preeminently exposed to German ideologies. Means should be found within the framework of the new world organisation to prevent the spreading of Fascist doctrines and other fallacies through school books and the press, which only arouse hostile sentiments towards other people.

The chauvinistic principle dominating these countries was responsible for creating an atmosphere inimical to healthy international co-operation of any kind. In view of this one of the first tasks of the democratic Hungarian Government was to revise all school textbooks. The aim of this revision was to eliminate all Fascist concepts and any statements which would cause antagonism toward our neighbours in the minds of our youths.

Furthermore, the Hungarian Government is planning the publication of a whole series of tracts emphasizing the common cultural and historical bonds between the Danubian peoples, which will also show that the economic co-operation between them is in the natural course of events.

Experiences of the past indicate the unhealthy Fascist morality, tendentiously spread through school books, the press and political publications and capable only of hatred of other people, is the most serious obstacle to firmly founded international co-operation.

The Hungarian Government thinks it desirable with this in mind to set up international cultural commissions within the framework of the new world organization—or at least limited to South-eastern Europe—which would undertake to investigate in a friendly spirit those biased statements and harmful tendencies appearing in the press, school books and political publications, which are liable to hamper international co-operation and good neighbourliness.

This commission could achieve positive constructive work by the promulgation of those tenets which would create a friendly atmosphere between the Danubian peoples. These principles could then be popularized by the different countries in their press, school books, and radio.

4. As for the territorial settlement to be undertaken by the peace conference, the Hungarian Government hopes to see established a peace "which will afford to all nations the means of dwelling in safety within their own boundaries, and which will afford assurance that all the men in all the lands may live out their lives in freedom from want and fear."

The conditions so wisely outlined in Article 6 of the Atlantic Charter can be realized only by the widest application of the principles of nationality. No doubt the ideal state of affairs would be if the boundaries would lose their significance. Failing this, the cause of international reconciliation and co-operation would best be served if nationalities living on contiguous territories were to belong to the same state.

The Hungarian people had to pay a heavy price for the failure to achieve this after the First World War, as largely due to this fact no sound democracy could be developed in Hungary. The Hungarian reactionaries for 25 years were sustained by the fact that one third of the Hungarian people torn away from the mother country against their will lived under severe oppression in the neighbouring countries. Hungarian public opinion could never understand why the Treaty of Trianon, advocating the principles of democracy and nationality, found it necessary to distribute one third of their compatriots among foreign states when the majority of them lived in one block on territories adjacent to Hungary. Hungarian minorities amounting to more than 3 millions unfortunately were subjected to the despotism of exaggerated nationalism, which fact was used to advantage by the reactionist Hungarian press to create and foster an irredentist and revisionist mentality in the Hungarian public.

The most effective measure to counteract national antagonism, which is still rampant in countries corrupted by Fascist doctrines and constantly stirred by chauvinist elements, would be the delimination of boundaries according to the freely expressed wish of the population and to the principles of nationality wherever the nationalities live on contiguous territories.

From the time of the French Revolution the principles of nationality as a basis for settlement have been universally accepted. This was the driving force behind several European revolutions. This principle inspired the theory of self-determination advocated by President Wilson and is the dominating feature of Lenin's and Stalin's works as well as of the constitution of the Soviet Union.

The Hungarian Government is well aware of the fact that a settlement according to the principles of nationality is not sufficient in itself to solve economic problems. The economic problems of South-eastern Europe cannot be eliminated by adjusting the boundaries one way or another but by extensive economic co-operation as mentioned in section 1. On the other hand if the boundaries are delineated in conformity with the wishes of the populations concerned this would bring about the political stability necessary to economic co-operation.

The idea of the transfer of population has been often suggested to facilitate the formation of homogeneous national states. The standpoint of the Hungarian Government is, in this respect, that the transfer of populations can be justified only when nationalities live in isolated fragmentary groups, that is to say, when it is impossible to reunite the national minorities with the mother country by redrawing the boundaries. What is more, such transfer of populations runs contrary to all rights of liberty as well as to the evolution of international law for the past 300 years, and can be considered as absolutely arbitrary in character. Major transfers of populations can be effected in the Danubian countries already overpopulated agriculturally only through corresponding territorial adjustments.

Finally, the Hungarian Government recalls that, as the example of the Greek-Turkish population transfer proves, such large-scale movements in population can be effected only by granting international credit and economic assistance. This is especially true in the case of Hungary, which is obliged to meet heavy reparation payments and considering that she has practically no transport facilities, her industries are in a deplorable state due to well known causes in connection with the war, furthermore, her agriculture cannot be expected to attain the prewar production level for five or six years due to the loss of 70 to 90 per cent of her live stock and to the radical land reform recently undertaken.

5. Since national minorities most probably will still be found outside the mother country however the borders may be drawn, it is absolutely necessary to provide for their protection by means of some international machinery of the United Nations.

The protection afforded to minorities by the League of Nations undoubtedly justified certain adverse criticism, but at least there was some protection. In many cases the very fact that such machinery existed was sufficient to restrain governments planning oppressive measures against minorities. It will be an act of retrogression if even such protection is not granted in the future to national minorities.

When presenting the above the Hungarian Government felt obliged to reciprocate the good will of the Powers at the Potsdam conference by joining actively the spiritual community of democratic nations and by participating unstintingly in their constructive work. The Hungarian Government is firmly convinced that at the time of the forthcoming international negotiations the strength of its proposals will be the fact that the Hungarian Government did not espouse any cause which is not in the common interest of all genuinely democratic countries. So the appreciation of the just and lawful Hungarian standpoint will serve not only Hungary but the cause of the sincere reconciliation of all European nations and thereby further the interests of world peace.

It is the earnest wish of the Hungarian nation that at last a peace should be concluded which in conformity with their wishes would take into consideration the just claims of all the peoples living along the banks of the Danube. A peace settlement based on justice and morality taking into account the legitimate interests and fundamental rights of peoples will bring tranquillity to the new world and will prevent another-world wide cataclysm.

I avail myself of this opportunity to renew to Your Excellency the expression of my highest consideration.

(signed) *Gyöngyösi.*

His Excellency
  A. D. F. Gascoigne, C. M. G.
  Political Representative of His Britannic Majesty's Government

His Excellency
  G. M. Puskin
  Envoy Extraordinary and Minister Plenipotentiary,
  Union of Socialist Soviet Republics

His Excellency
  H. F. Arthur Schoenfeld
  Envoy Extraordinary and Minister Plenipotentiary,
  United States Representative in Hungary,

Budapest.

Hungarian Ministry for Foreign Affairs.

DOCUMENT NO. 12

Budapest, November, 12th 1945.

100/res/Be.

_____

1945.

Sir,

For kind transmission to the Government of the United Stated States of America,

His Britannic Majesty's Government,

I have the honour to transmit herewith the enclosed memorandum detailing the position of the Hungarian Government concerning water routes giving access to the sea, and problems connected with the hydrographic unity of the Carpathian Basin.

The interests of world peace, as well as considerations to promote the economic welfare of the Danubian nations and their friendly cooperation, equally necessitate that these questions should be settled at the Peace Conference in the most complete and efficient manner. The memorandum of the Hungarian Government intends to be a modest contribution and participation in the expert preparation of the great work of the Peace Conference for a permanent consolidation of world peace.

Sir, I avail myself of this opportunity to renew to Your Excellency the expression of my highest consideration.

(signed) _Gyöngyösi_

His Excellency
G. M. Puskin
Envoy Extraordinary, Minister Plenipotentiary,
Union of Socialist Soviet Republics,

His Excellency
H. F. Arthur Schoenfeld,
Envoy Extraordinary, Minister Plenipotentiary,
United States Representative in Hungary,

His Excellency
A. D. F. Gascoigne, C. M. G.
Political Representative of His Britannic Majesty's Government

Budapest.

MEMORANDUM

of the Hungarian Government relating to the free access to the sea, and to the solution of problems arising from the hydrographic unity of the Carpathian Basin

The Hungarian Government—in their Note No. 44/res/Be.—1945, dated August 14th, 1945, and addressed to the Powers assembled at Potsdam—referred to a few points of view which will have to be considered in order to secure a prosperous future for the various nations living along the Danube. Besides certain general principles, the reasonable and serviceable solution of some groups of practical problems is a common interest of all nations in the Danube valley, and entirely independent of how political questions will be settled.

Problems of such a nature are those connected with the following: free access to the sea, water-exploitation in the Carpathian Basin forming a hydrographic unity, protection against floods, and harnessing and utilizing water energy.

There can be no doubt that peace in the future largely depends on the ability of mankind to employ their highly developed craft in promoting reconstruction and increasing prosperity, instead of destruction and devastation. This is especially the case in respect of those countries of South-Eastern Europe which possess no sea ports and cannot, therefore, avail themselves of the rapidly developing and inexpensive water transport facilities unless they are entitled to do so by means of international conventions. Similarly, international conventions are indispensable both for utilizing the immense power of the waters in the Carpathian Basin—forming a hydrographic unity cut up by political frontiers—and for mastering their destructive forces and putting them into the service of an increased production.

Regarding these questions, the Hungarian Government are desirous of exposing their views as follows.

I.
THE PROBLEM OF ENSURING FREE ACCESS TO THE SEA

Three of the countries situated on the Danube viz.: Hungary, Austria, and Czechoslovakia cannot reach the sea except by the Danube, or overland. The aggregate population of these three countries amounts to about 30 millions, a considerable number of people interested in the question of free access to the sea. Of course, the Hungarian Government do not feel competent to state the views of Austria and Czechoslovakia; owing to their geographic situation, the views of these countries may be divergent in many respects from those of Hungary, Accordingly, they limit their investigation to their own point of view.

1. The Danube waterway.

The river Danube, which flows through Hungary, empties into the Black Sea from where, by way of the Bosphorus and the Dardanelles, there is a free sea-route to the Mediterranean and the Oceans.

Thus the river Danube is the only natural waterway for Hungary to reach the sea in a direct way by means of Hungarian vessels.

The length of the Danube route is 1428 kilometres from the southern frontier of Hungary to the Black Sea, and 1647 kilometres from Budapest to the Black Sea. Taking an average height of the Danube water level, single crafts (motor-ships for combined Danube and sea service) would require 80 hours of actual passage down stream, and 160 hours up-stream.

Pre-requisite to the use of this natural and favourable route are international conventions ensuring and facilitating the freedom of navigation on the Danube and on its navigable tributaries as well as international organs permanently superintending the carrying out of such conventions.

For the last 25 years the freedom of navigation on the Danube — as regards free access to the sea — has been prevalent. Its pledges were:

a. The peace treaties of Paris (Articles 275 and 276 of the Treaty of Trianon as well as the corresponding articles of the other peace treaties) declaring the Danube to be international from Ulm to the Black Sea and open to all flags on a footing of complete equality.

b. The Danube Convention concluded at Paris on the 23rd of July, 1921 (ratified by Hungary by Act No. 14 of 1923) with a view to establishing definite regulation concerning the Danube. Article I of this Convention provides that "navigation is to be unrestricted and open to all flags, on a footing of perfect equality, on the entire navigable portion of the Danube i.e. from Ulm to the Black Sea".

c. According to Article III of the Convention the freedom of navigation and the equality of flags are secured by two Commissions *viz.* the International Danube Commission on the fluvial Danube (Ulm-Braila) and the European Danube Commission on the maritime Danube (Braila-River-mouth).

Article X provides that the International Danube Commission has to see that there is no impediment, by any act of any state, to the freedom of navigation, further, that the principle of equal treatment is applied to transport and harbour facilities, to the equipments and installations of the ports and, in general, that there is no detriment to the international character of the Danube system declared to be international by conventions.

Considering that the Danube Convention and the two Commissions named above were adequate to secure duly the freedom of navigation on the Danube, for maintaining this freedom for the future it would seem necessary:

1. To put into operation again the Danube Convention with the necessary modifications.

2. To reinstate—merged into one if possible—the International Danube Commission and the European Danube Commission.

As long as the principle of freedom of navigation prevails, access to the sea for vessels flying the Hungarian flag is free and direct. The capacity of the Danube waterway is practically unlimited for all kinds of goods. Freights can be fixed uninfluenced by any foreign state if the transport is effected by Hungarian vessels.

In case of transports on the Danube by river craft, to or from the sea, transhipments between seagoing vessels and barges cannot be made at the mouth of the river (Sulina) where there is no equipment suitable for this purpose but they must take place in one of the great Roumanian river-harbours, either at Galatz or at Braila.

Galatz and Braila are situated respectively 150 and 171 kilometres from the mouth of the river. Seagoing vessels can reach these harbours on the Sulina branch.

Cargo, if not transhipped directly from a seagoing vessel on to a river craft or vice versa, may be handled (transhipped) at both these places in harbours belonging to the state.

Experience in the past has proved that such a method involves difficulties, considerable expense, and therefore it would be desirable and expedient to allow free zones in these harbours for Hungarian cargoes.

The Hungarian combined Danubian-maritime navigation has special advantages for Hungary inasmuch as it makes possible the sending out of Hungarian goods to the ports of the Near East, or imports from these ports, in a direct way, without transhipping and at freight charges that can be paid in Hungarian currency, and which are in keeping with Hungarian economic interests. This is of immense importance for Hungary, considering the great difficulties she will have to face in the foreign exchange market, if not permanently but, at any rate, for a number of years to come.

2. Ensuring the overland route to the sea.

One of the overland routes to the sea is the railway built at enormous cost by the Hungarian Government with a view to linking up Fiume, at that time Hungarian port on the Adriatic Sea.

Hungary has been entirely cut off from the sea by the provisions of the Trianon Treaty concluded after the first world war, severing Fiume, and a great part of the overland route leading to this place, from the rest of the country.

Realizing probably that Hungary, cut off from the sea, could hardly survive, Article 294 of the Treaty of Trianon provides as follows: "Free access to the Adriatic Sea is accorded to Hungary who with this object will enjoy freedom of transit over the territories and in the ports severed from the former Austro-Hungarian-Monarchy". The same article stipulates that "special conventions between the States and Administrations concerned will lay down the conditions of the exercise of the right accorded above".

This proviso declares, in principle, the right to the free use of, and access to, the sea ports without however giving instructions for putting it into practice, nor does it provide for the event of one or the other of the states in possession impeding or frustrating the use of the ports, or of the railways leading to them, by means of covert measures.

Such a covert impediment was, on the part of the foreign railway companies sharing in transit, their attitude denying the application of the tariff transit-trade, which would have served Hungarian economic interests, and persistently charged the higher rates of their internal tariffs established to meet entirely different interests. The direct result of such an attitude was that—though reductions of a certain per cent for Hungarian goods had been allowed in the meantime—the combined tariff in the Hungarian—Adriatic Sea Port relation, so vitally important for the oversea traffic of Hungary, could not be made operative until March 1st, 1928 i.e. 8 years after the ratification of the peace treaty. It need hardly be explained how detrimental to the economic life of Hungary the loss of these 8 years was. The necessarily growing interest of Hungary for the northern sea ports and her increasing orientation towards the German sphere of influence were partially due to the lack of free access to the Adriatic.

While in the beginning, after the first world war, Hungarian railway traffic tended towards the Adriatic, with the passing of the years, owing to the reasons mentioned above, it gradually changed its course towards the northern and eastern sea ports. It is characteristic that while Hungarian trade in the Adriatic ports in 1935 amounted to 98,000 tons as compared with 78,000 tons in the German ports, in 1936 these figures changed into 112,800 tons and 149,800 tons respectively in favour of the German ports.

Free zones in the ports of both the Adriatic and the eastern and northern seas will be an absolute necessity for Hungary in the future as well as they have been in the past. Further, unrestricted use of the railway lines leading to these ports, at reasonable tariffs, will have to be secured for her. In order to settle the questions concerning railway rates it would be best to insert a clause in the peace treaty *authorizing Hungary to apply her own tariffs* all the way to the seaports. The railways of the transit states would share in the freights in the ratio of their services.

If such a solution, fair to all states concerned, could not be accepted, the combined tariffs which used to be operative on the lines between Hungary and the Adriatic before the second world war, should be made permanent as a maximum for her traffic both with the Adriatic and with the eastern and northern seaports.

Apart from Fiume, it would be desirable for the Adriatic traffic of Hungary to have the use of the port of Trieste secured for her as well.

Thanks to its larger and better installations, and to the greater tonnage available there, the port of Trieste is in many cases preferable to that of Fiume, whereas the difference between the two as regards distances (and tariffs) is negligible, the respective routes being 622 kilometres for Budapest—Gyékényes—Zagreb—Fiume, 633 kilometres for Budapest—Murakeresztur—Postumia—Fiume, and 642 kilometres for Budapest—Murakeresztur—Postumia—Trieste.

It may be added that the Karlovac—Fiume portion of the route Budapest—Gyékényes—Karlovac—Fiume, leading through the

Karst region, is rather difficult to work, but this can be avoided by using the Budapest—Murakeresztur—Postumia—S. Pietro del Carso route i.e. the same which leads to Trieste too.

3. Facilitating water transport by means of international conventions.

For maintaining to the full satisfaction of all participants navigation on the Danube, which is crossing or touching the territories of eight riparian states, co-operation of these states is an absolute necessity.

The general principles of such a co-operation are laid down in the Danubian Convention and the reconstructed Danube Commission will have to see that these principles are enforced. In addition there are numerous minor problems of navigation on the Danube the uniform and satisfactory solution of which—by means of agreements between the riparian states—would result in facilitating transport considerably.

These problems to be solved by international arrangements are of technical, legal, administrative and other nature and, without going into particulars, may be summarily sketched as follows:

a) *Technical problems.*

In order to solve the problems arising from the hydrographic unity of the Danube Basin constituting a complete river system, and to maintain a regular hydrometric and flood prognosticating service, it is imperative to set up a commission composed of the representants of all riparian states, similar to the Danubian Permanent Hydraulic Technical Commission (CRED).

The Hungarian Government find it necessary to point out once again that this Commission (CRED) called into existence by Article 293 of the Trianon Treary did very useful and long-needed work, and that its activity has been of special importance to Hungary extending as it does along the middle course of the streams rushing down from the Carpathians. The undisturbed service mentioned before is of extreme importance both from the point of view of flood prognostication service and in the interests of navigation.

Further, it would be desirable to lay down uniform regulations regarding the fitness and safety of the vessels, and for providing them with life-preserving appliances. Finally, there is a pressing need to establish a network of telephone (or radio) service along the Danube connecting the head-offices of the shipping companies with their executive organs at all times.

b) *Legal problems.*

The League of Nations took the steps in 1922 towards making the law concerning inland navigation uniform in various river systems by referring the question of unifying the inland navigation laws to a committee called "Comité pour l'unification du Droit Fluvial". A Hungarian expert was to collaborate with them.

The Committee prepared 3 draft conventions in the course of a few years. The first of these, under the heading *"Draft Convention relating to the regulation of questions of the navigation-laws"* aimed at settling the following questions: the compulsory registration of inland water vessels; ownership; mortgages; privileges; execution. The second of the Drafts, under the heading *"Draft Convention relating to suitable administrative measures for certifying the nationality of inland vessels"* serves the regulation, within certain limits, of the nationality of vessels. The third of them, under the heading *"Draft Convention relating to the unification of certain regulations concerning the collisions occurring in inland navigation"* aims at the regulation of questions arising from the collisions of inland water vessels.

It is desirable that the questions treated in these draft conventions, as well as those whose legal unification appears to be useful, should be settled at last by means of international discussions.

c) *Administrative problems, and various other questions.*

When settling again the Danube questions, the separate examinations at the frontier-stations of two neighbouring states should be, in the interests of expediting navigation, united and executed, at a common station simultaneously by the organs of both states concerned. To expedite examinations: uniform principles, formalities and dues in customs houses and harbours should also be introduced instead of varying in each country as hitherto.

Another important task still to be accomplished is the drawing up of up-to-date trade statistics based on identical principles. Danube statistics in the past were hardly suitable for the purpose of making international comparisons, for each riparian state did the compiling and publishing of data according to its own adopted system.

With regard to the safety of traffic, uniform qualifications of the pilots would be necessary. The frequent and constant intercourse between the Danube boatmen makes it advisable to regulate on the same lines in all riparian states the work and leisure hours, and the leave of absence on pay of the crews, and to introduce uniform ship service books. Finally, uniform sanitary and veterinary regulations should be agreed upon.

It is worth mentioning that in Article XL of the Danube Convention all signatory powers undertook to agree, by means of special conventions, upon uniform legal, commercial, sanitary and veterinary rules concerning navigation and transport contracts, but this has not been realised for the last 25 years.

4. Conclusions.

Based upon the remarks set forth above, the Hungarian Government would sum up their requests relating to a free access to the sea in the following conclusions.

1. Putting into operation again the Danube Convention with the necessary modifications.

2. Reinstating the International Danube Commission and the European Danube Commission, the two merged into one if possible.

3. Securing free zones for Hungarian cargoes in the harbours of Galatz and Braila, considering that otherwise the handling (transhipping) of goods involves difficulties, a good deal of expense and loss of time.

4. Securing free zones in the ports of both the Adriatic and the eastern and northern seas.

5. Securing reduced railway tariffs, viz.:

a) Provisions authorizing Hungary to apply her own tariffs all the way to the sea ports, yet with a clause to the effect that the railways of the transit states would share in the freights in the ratio of their services.

b) If such a solution, fair to all states concerned, could not be accepted, the combined tariffs which were operating on the lines between Hungary and the Adriatic before the second world war should be made permanent as a maximum for her traffic both with the Adriatic and with the eastern and northern sea-ports.

6. Facilitating water transport by means of international conventions, namely:

a) Establishing a Danubian hydraulic-technical commission composed of the delegates of all riparian states.

b) Uniform regulations regarding the fitness and safety of vessels, and for providing them with life-preserving appliances, and further, establishing a network of telephone (or radio) service along the Danube.

c) Unifying the inland navigation laws as started by the League of Nations.

d) Establishing common frontier stations where the examinations could be made simultaneously by the organs of both states concerned. To expedite examinations at the frontiers, uniform principles, formalities and dues in customs houses and harbours should be introduced instead of varying in each state as hitherto.

e) It would be necessary for the riparian states to conclude an agreement with a view to drawing up and publishing up-to-date statistics based on identical principles.

f) With regard to the safety of the traffic, uniform qualifications of the pilots and the introduction of uniform ship service books by all riparian states would be desirable. From the point of view of the welfare of the crews, it would be advisable to regulate on the same lines their work and leisure hours and their leave of absence on pay.

g) In general, it would be desirable to provide, by means of international conventions, for uniform legal, commercial, sanitary and veterinary rules concerning navigation and transport contracts as proposed by Article XL of the Danube Statute.

SOLUTION OF PROBLEMS ARISING FROM THE HYDROGRAPHIC UNITY OF THE CARPATHIAN BASIN.

1. Hydrographic situation of Hungary.

From a hydrographic point of view, the Carpathian Basin is a closed geologic, resp. geographic formation, complete in itself, in which all streams—with the exception of the Danube forming its axis and of a few small tributaries rising in the Alps, and further, of the rivers Aluta (Olt) and Dunajec—are rising, flowing in the entire length of their course, and emptying within this basin.

Hungary herself is situated at the bottom of the Carpathian Basin with the result that, apart from the rivers, all the rain and snow falling within the ridges of the Carpathians gather on her territory. Consequently, there is hardly any part of the Hungarian plain which—due to its hydrographic situation—would not be affected by the danger of damages caused by water, or which could not be improved by the utilization of its waters.

The energies latent in the waters are working incessantly; they try to re-inundate, and convert into swamps, such regions as have already been made safe by means of appropriate works, river regulating constructions and dikes; they may cause greater destruction and more terrible catastrophes than any other force of nature.

40% of Hungary is wheat-growing territory, and 33% of all her arable land lies in the river inundation areas. These two data alone suffice to characterize the significance of the Hungarian water problems, and to indicate the extraordinary importance of the protection against floods.

There can be no doubt about the necessity of such measures as are adequate, in the fight against the destructions of the water, to remove the dangers threatening the work of protection which, owing to political circumstances, may prove ineffective.

2. Protection against floods.

The work of protection in Hungary against damages caused by floods may be called considerably advanced.

It is estimated by political economists that, as a result of the work of protection against floods, performed on a vast scale on the territory of pre-first-world-war Hungary at a cost amounting to nearly one and a half billion gold Pengös (292 million dollars), the national wealth of Hungary has increased by 6 billion gold Pengös (1.2 billion dollars).

As to its dimensions, the Hungarian flood protection system was the largest in Europe. Dikes of an aggregate length of nearly 6,400 kilometres have protected in 1918 a territory of 3,700,000 hectares in Hungary, i.e. larger than the entire territory of Holland.

A considerable part of this protected territory, i.e. 2,300,000 hectares, has remained in present Hungary, the rest being now beyond the Trianon frontier which severed the flood area of 24 water companies. This fact made it necessary for Hungary, in her continual fight against the damages caused by water, to multiply her efforts beyond all that she had done in work and expenses in the past.

Hungary, situated at the bottom of the Carpathian basin, constitutes a natural reservoir for all waters flowing into this basin. The separated areas of the severed water companies are on the upper course of the streams with the result that they are in a considerably more favourable position than the territories which have remained under Hungarian sovereignty. Namely, whenever the flood, at a place beyond the Hungarian frontier, overflows the dikes, or in case there is a breach in the dikes, or they get broken on purpose, the Hungarian territories are bound to become flooded. In the same way, stagnant waters from beyond the frontier may inundate the protected Hungarian territories if their pumping is neglected, or their gradual damming up which was a rule in the past is not effected, or the canals are not dredged properly on the territories annexed to the neighbouring states.

All these damages repeatedly occurred during the period from 1919 up to the present, and the Hungarian parts of the companies suffered severe losses either by the prevention of damages, or more frequently by the impossibility of preventing them. It is obvious that the parts of the companies beyond the frontiers would suffer in the same way, if the Hungarian part constructed dikes at the frontiers as a protection against damages of such a kind.

The frontiers as fixed by the Trianon Treaty deprived Hungary of even the possibility of diminishing the mass of waters rushing down from the mountains, by means of rational afforestation. Hungary's forestry policy in the past considered as its principal object to keep intact her forests extending to 7,500,000 hectares, and to reduce the bare areas under 2.5% (185,000 hectares) of the afforested area. By means of reafforestation and by tying up the gullies the coarse fragments could be retained to such an extent that nothing but sand and mud were carried along by the Hungarian navigable rivers in their middle and lower courses.

In order to preserve the beneficial effects produced by the forests which have the properties of retaining rain and snow, of tying up the soil, and of influencing the level of the floods, it would be necessary to have an international body dealing with the technical problems of the hydrographic system in the Carpathian Basin.

Considering that the protection against the destructive effects of the floods is common concern, when fixing the frontiers it would be advisable to pay regard—as far as ethnographic, economic and other considerations allow it—to the hydrographic unity determined by ridges forming watersheds, or at least to see that the frontiers do not sever the unity of water companies.

3. Water-exploitation.

The natural forces hidden in the formerly devastating watercourses, once harnessed by means of regulation and protection against floods, may be employed in the service of useful economic work.

a) *Utilization of Water power.*

There are numerous valleys on the inner slopes of the Carpathians surrounding the Hungarian Basin situated favourably for storing in them large masses of water very economically. Especially the valleys of the Teresva (Tarac), Tereblja (Talabor), Rika (Nagyàg), Tiecna (Técsâ), Visaul (Visô) and Iza in the North-Eastern Carpathians, and those of the Jad (Jàd), Dragan (Dragàn) and Bistra (Bisztra) in the Bihar Erzgebirge are offering possibilities of storing water which could be utilized in five different ways viz.: producing water power, securing water for the purpose of navigation when the level is low, providing water for irrigation, supplying water for drinking and industrial purposes, and finally, reducing dangerous flood levels. These possibilities are eminently suitable for solving the water-economy problems of the Great Hungarian Plain.

Preliminary studies of Hungarian experts estimate the storing capacity of the 15 valleys in the North-Eastern Carpathians at 10—900 million cubic metres. The Visaul (Visô) valley power station alone could produce 160 million kilowatts of energy annually.

b) *Irrigation Works.*

The climatic conditions of the Hungarian Plain are, in general, favourable for agriculture but they do not always secure the quantity of water necessary in the period of production. For instance, the rainfall—as shown by the average of many years—in the centre of the Plain, from the 1st of April to the 30th of September does not exceed 300 millimetres, insufficient even for the purpose of extensive cultivation.

For this reason, i.e. in order to better ensure the conditions of production and to increase production both in volume and in value, Hungary began in 1937 the construction of irrigation works on an area of 200,000 hectares. The economic importance of the irrigation is best shown by the fact that besides cereals, yielding very irregularly, fodder, vegetables, rice, oil-yielding, leguminous and industrial plants will be produced on the territories in question.

One hectare of unirrigated soil, in the usual rotation of crops, produced in Hungary mixed produce amounting to 50 quintals, having a nourishment value of 6 million calories. The same territory, if irrigated, may be expected to yield 140 quintals of mixed produce, with a nourishment value of 15 million calories. The large irrigation works have also social effects inasmuch as they are going to supply with better and more food 750,000 people instead of 300,000 as before, i.e. the multiple by two and a half, and to give employment and bread to four to five times as many workmen than did the arid economy. By sufficient irrigation-water the irrigated territory may be incrased to 6–700,000 hectares some time in the future, which involves better nourishment for 2–2.5 million people and more employment for a very considerable mass of workmen.

Alcaline territories in Hungary still to be improved may be estimated at 500,000 hectares. Production can be increased on these too with the help of appropriate water economy. Alcaline basins entirely unfit for production could be turned into fisheries. Up to the present 200 fish-ponds have already been established, on 10,000 hectares of mostly alcaline soil.

c) *The importance of Waterways.*

Hungary's activities during the last hundred years in the interest of improving navigation and conditions of water flow, and also of stabilizing river beds have been very remarkable. At cost amounting to round one billion gold Pengös (200 million dollars)* she regulated in the Danube valley, besides the Danube itself, the rivers Drava (Dràva), Sava (Szàva), Kupa (Kulpa), Morava (Morva), Vàk (Vàg) and Timis (Temes), and in the Tisza valley, besides the Tisza itself, the rivers Bodrog, Mures (Maros) and Somes (Szamos). She has constructed artificial waterways, viz. the canal-system

---

*Calculated at the rate of exchange of P.5. 13 to $1 in 1938, premium included.

called Kanal Kralje Petra (Ferenc csatorna), the Bega, the Soroksàr branch of the Danube and the Kris (Körös); constructions for rendering the Sió and Sajó navigable are being made as well as the main irrigation canal between the rivers Tisza and Berettyó which will be accessible to our largest river craft. Further, it is planned to construct in the near future a navigation canal between the Danube and the Tisza.

The linking up, in an intensive way, of the Tisza valley with the Danube navigation would help this rather neglected region to great prosperity, to be increased still by the fact that the transport by water would promote the favourable marketing of the surplus production to be arrived at by the help of the irrigation works on the Great Plain. It is estimated that as soon as the Danube-Tisza canal is available, the farmer may save 10–15% of the value of his production by using the waterway instead of the railway. It is a well known fact that the cost of transport by water is about $1/3$–$1/4$ part of that by railway.

The Trianon Treaty and the Danube Statute declared the Danube, under the control of the International Danube Commission, to be international from Ulm to Braila,—the Tisza from the mouth of the Somes (Szamos), the Drava (Dràva) from Barcs, the Mures (Maros) from Arad, to their mouths. The navigable branches of these rivers have also been declared international. In principle, those navigable waters have been declared international "which naturally provide more than one state with access to the sea". However, the Bega, the Timis (Temes) and the Kanal Kralja Petra (Ferenc-csatorna) have not been declared international in spite of the fact that the way from them to the sea has to lead through more than one state, and that they constitute an organic part of the water system in the Carpathian Basin.

It was in 1856 that the Treaty of Paris declared navigation to be free. Hungary had already declared the levying of duty on the rivers to be illegal much earlier, by Act No. XV in 1723; Act No. XVII of the year 1737 forbids, under the penalty of 100 gold florins, the levying of any kind of dues on ships and rafts communicating on natural waterways.

True to this principle adopted more than two hundred years ago, in the interest of the freedom of navigation, and in order to enable all parties participating in navigation to acquire all economic benefits due to them, the Hungarian Government think it desirable that all navigable tributaries in the Danube valley as well as canals linked up with them be declared to be international, on a footing of mutuality and reciprocity.

4. Provisions of the Trianon Treaty and experience gained by them.

Besides the International Danube Commission mentioned above there was, operating between Braila and the mouths of the Danube, the European Danube Commission on which Hungory has not been represented in spite of her sharing, to a considerable extent, in the traffic of maritime Danube.

The third international organization was the Danubian Permanent Hydraulic Technical Commission, also mentioned above, called into existence at the request of Hungary by Article 293 of the Trianon Treaty for the purpose of settling in an international way questions of a hydraulic technical nature, or those of forestry connected with them, arising in the Carpathian Basin from the frontiers as fixed by the Treaty. In some cases, especially when aided by the good-will of the parties concerned, the Commission succeeded in furthering the solution of grave problems; in other cases, however, they failed with a considerable part of the questions put before them.

Taught by experience, and in order to simplify administration which has been rather intricate with the three different international commissions, it would be advisable to have a single commission only, with competence extended from the mouth at the Black Sea to the highest navigable point of the Danube at Ulm, as well as on all navigable tributaries, branches and navigation canals linked up with the Danube.

The functions of the Danubian Permanent Technical Commission should be transferred to a technical sub-commission of an International Danube Commission to be set up for this purpose and also for dealing with questions arising from the hydraulic conditions of Hungary, with her cooperation if possible, and by means of conventions to be concluded with the neighbouring states.

Further, it would be necessary to secure for Hungary the right of erecting on the territory of a neighbouring state such water storing and power producing works as are absolutely necessary for the economic development of the Great Hungarian Plain (e.g. for the construction of irrigation works on the Plain) and cannot be constructed on the territory of Hungary; or, in case such works are erected by the neighbouring state itself, to ensure, by means of agreements, for Hungary, the supply of the volume of water or energy which is necessary for her purpose (e.g. the construction of the Danube-Tisza Canal, or the rendering of the Moson branch of the Danube navigable). Finally, a long-term international loan would be desirable for the construction of water storing and power producing works of public interest in the Carpathian Basin.

5. Economic background of the hydraulic questions.

It is obvious that the hydrographic unity of the Carpathian Basin has been disrupted by the Trianon Treaty. The river Tisza alone touches the territories of four states. All the possible water storing places in the mountainous regions, suitable for reducing the damages done by floods, and for supplying us with irrigation water, with cheap power, and water for navigation at times when our rivers are drying up, are on territories under the sovereignty of the neighbouring states. The Hungary of Trianon has been left with the lower regions only so critical from the point of view of protection against flood.

In such a situation the importance of our hydraulic problems increased considerably, and any omission on our part would injure our national economy to a greater extent than before 1918.

Navigation is one of the most important factors of our economic life. The inexpensive transport by water not only linking up with the Adriatic and the Black Sea, but also the development of our river navigation and of a navigable river system. Our produce cannot be able to compete unless we can secure the advantages of transport by water to as high a degree as possible.

This requirement is growing in intensity for another reason too, viz, it is only by making use of the inexpensive water transport that we can turn to our advantage the surplus of production which may be expected both in quantity and in quality as a result of the irrigation works begun on the Great Plain. Our agriculture is affected by the cost of transport to a higher degree than is the case with industrial production; for its marketable goods, larger both in quantity and in volume, the most natural means of transport is that by water. In 1940 64% of our wheat export and 67% of our flour export was transported by water.

The development of our intensive agricultural production cannot be ensured unless our system of protection against floods, built at enormous cost, can fulfil in an undisturbed way, and safe from external surprises, its task of protecting our agriculture from the damages by water, due to our geographic and climatic situation.

Irrigation, navigation and power production are alike prominent factors of water-utilization. Nevertheless, the Preparatory Committee of the Barcelona Conference decided in 1921 that in case of a collision between the interests of navigation and other matters relating to water, priority should be given, even to the prejudice of navigation, to the best way of water-utilization. It is in this sense that the Hungarian Government request the international ensurance of their water-utilization projects.

6. The necessity of immediate measures.

Pending the international regulation by Treaties of Peace of the problems sketched above, it is imperative to set up a provisional international body for settling hydraulic problems arising, as it were, day by day, or at least to entitle the Hungarian Government, in cases of emergency, to get in direct touch with the neighbouring states, by permission and under control of the Allied Control Commission.

7. Conclusions.

In accordance with the above reflections, the Hungarian Government are desirous of submitting the following requests relating to the solution of problems arising from the hydrographic unity of the Carpathian Basin dismembered by political frontiers:

1. The frontiers could be best fixed by paying regard to the hydrographic unity determined by ridges forming watersheds, in every case when ethnical or important economic considerations do not preclude such an adjustment. In any case care should

be taken that the unity of water-companies is not severed by frontiers.

2. The Hungarian Government thinks it desirable that every navigable tributary and canal in the Danube valley shall be declared to be international on the footing of reciprocity and mutuality.

3. The regulation of all technical questions arising from the severing, by political frontiers, of the Carpathian Basin forming a hydrographic unity, should be subjected to the competence of the Danubian Permanent Hydraulic Technical Committee which could be reorganized as a technical sub-committee, set up for this purpose, of the United International Danube Commission. This Committee should have the power, e.g. to order reasonable forest culture with a view to eliminating damages done to the entire water system of the Carpathian Basin by inexpert management of the forests. In a similar way, this committee should superintend the water-companies for the prevention of floods severed by, or situated in the neigh-bourhood of political frontiers, and should also see that no catas-trophe is caused by omitting the preventive measures.

4. Further, it would be necessary to authorize, by means of international agreements, the Hungarian state to erect on the territory of a neighbouring state such water-storing and power-producing works as are indispensable for the economic develop-ment of Hungarian areas in the Plain. In case such works are erected by the neighbouring state, the supply to Hungary of the necessary volume of water and power should be ensured by interna-tional agreements. Finally, international long-term loans would be desirable for the purpose of constructing water-storing and power-producing works serving the interests of the community.

5. Pending the definite international regulation of the problems sketched above, it would be necessary to set up a provisional international body for the purpose of solving such hydraulic prob-lems as arise now day by day—or at least, to authorize the Hungarian Government to get in direct touch with the neighbouring states in case of emergency.

SECRET* DOCUMENT NO. 13

LONDON   2 May 1946 6 pm
                                          330
SECRET   3 May 9 am

In letter dated April 30 Foreign Office reported recent conversations between Gascoigne and Hungarian Prime Minister. Sense of Foreign Office letter is as follows:

When Nagy was asked for his views on recent political developments in Hungary, he at once endeavored to justify any concessions which his Government had made to demands of Hungarian Communist Party. He stated that Smallholders Party had been in very weak position to resist demands made on them for following reasons. Soviets had been extremely displeased with Hungary because of her reluctance to sign agreement for economic collaboration and for backwardness in reparation deliveries. His Party was in a weak position morally because certain of its members had been behaving in a "reactionary" manner, "making tactless statements, which were offensive to Russian authorities". Nagy had been confronted with danger of finding his Government abandoned by other members of coalition, with a consequent outbreak of riots and strikes. The result would have been a loss in governmental control as the police force could not be counted on to maintain order.

Embassy will remember late in March both United States and British Governments instructed their representatives in Budapest that, if their opinions were sought, they might inform members of Hungarian Government that view of our two governments is that policy of maintaining coalition at all costs was of questionable wisdom and that continued concessions to a minority group would only end in the negation of people's mandate expressed at recent elections.

Gascoigne, acting in sense of these restrictions, replied to Nagy that he hoped he would not make further concessions to Left, and also pointed out that predominant position of Smallholders Party would be lost and the mandate acquired at elections thrown away. Gascoigne concluded by saying that British Government took very real interest in seeing establishment in Hungary of truly demo-

*Box 96, RG-32, N.A.

cratic regime based on popular will. Inasmuch as Nagy had not specifically asked for British Government's views, Gascoigne gave above as his personal opinions and not those of British Government.

Nagy expressed his appreciation and said knowledge of British Government's interest would give Hungarian Government more confidence for future. "He stated twice over that he would refuse to make any further concessions in regard to make up of Smallholders Party."

In reporting conversation Gascoigne said he believed that in spite of this reply Nagy was obsessed with the necessity of keeping on good terms with USSR.

From a further conversation since Nagy's return from Moscow it appears Soviet attitude to Hungarian requests was sympathetic and that they did not ask for anything from Hungary. "Nagy may now therefore be feeling a bit braver and your Government may care to consider whether they, too, could not usefully send him an encouraging message." British are not in a position, however, to offer him concrete assistance but it is in favor of doing anything possible to show interest in a real democratic regime and to encourage Smallholders to stand up to Communist minority.

Embassy will also remember that on March 2, Kennan presented formal letter to Molotov expressing dissatisfaction with state of economic affairs in Hungary and suggesting that three Allied Commissioners in Budapest should concert together before March 15 to devise satisfactory economic program. Similarly British Charge in Moscow on March 11 sent Molotov a supporting letter. "These letters have so far as we know had no result whatever." On other hand, there is a continued deterioration of whole economic life of Hungary; and furthermore Hungarian Government has now signed agreement for setting up Soviet economic combines for control of navigation of Danube, oil, bauxite, and airways. "Should be interested to know whether your Government which took the initiative in this matter is considering any step to follow the matter up."

This concludes sense of Foreign Office letter.

May we inform Foreign Office of Vyshinski's reply of April 21 to Kennan's letter of March 2 as transmitted in Moscow's 1302, April 23?

HARRIMAN

DOCUMENT NO. 14

DIVISION OF
COMMUNICATIONS AND RECORDS
TELEGRAPH BRANCH

DEPARTMENT OF STATE   **ACTION COPY**

INCOMING TELEGRAM

ACTION-TRO——
INFO:
A-C
EUR
NEA
DC/L
ITP
FC
DC/R

JSP -C-N
Paraphrase before com-
municating to anyone.

SECRET

SECSTATE

PRIORITY

871, May 9, (?)

MYTEL 774, April 25.

4439

Budapest

Dated May 9, 1946

Rec'd 9:30 a.m., 12th

711.6427/4-254

Kertesz of FOROFF told me today FORMIN desired me to
know privately and unofficially that Russians are taking
very stiff opposition line re operational landing rights
for American aircraft. Pushkin argues that inasmuch as
it is unthinkable that Soviet aircraft would be granted
such rights in American Zone in Germany or in Italy and
since Russian aircraft have allegedly been shot down
in American Zone, Soviet Government is not willing to
permit aircraft to fly (presumably without Russian clearance in each case) in any zone under Soviet control.
Pushkin reportedly added that American aircraft would not
be permitted to fly operationally in areas such as Hungary
within five hours flying time of Moscow.

Kertesz emphasized this was an authorized intimation
from Gyongyosi and that Hungarian Government is completely
at loss to answer our note requesting landing rights which
is admittedly reasonable and logically correct.

Sent Dept, repeated London as 217, Berlin as 53,
Moscow as 198, and Paris for Secretary as 129.

DES

SECRET

OFFICE OF TRANSPORT
AND COMMUNICATIONS
POLICY

MESSAGE UNSIGNED

MAY 1

DEPARTMENT OF STATE

PERMANENT RECORD COPY: THIS COPY MUST BE RETURNED TO DC/R CENTRAL FILES WITH
NOTATION OF ACTION TAKEN.

SECRET*   **DOCUMENT NO. 15**   Index *4680*

Dec: HTM mjd

BUDAPEST	July 9, 1946 Lam
	202
SECRET	July 11, 1946

Repeating our 1084 of June 7, 2pm.

"We learn from Karasz that Gyongyosi yesterday requested clearance for Karasz trip to Paris as peace delegate but Pushkin was reluctant stating he had had difficulties with Moscow after clearing Kertesz (My telegram 874 May 9th). Pushkin suggested that if Karasz were invited he could obtain a clearance easily. Gyongyosi pointed out in probability of such invitation and reiterated his request which Pushkin said he would have to take up with his Government."

Sent Department repeated to Paris for US DEL CEM as 202 and Moscow as 225.

SCHOENFELD

---

*Box 97, RG-43, N.A.

B.
The Transylvanian Question and the Hungarian Government's Visit to Moscow (April 9 to April 18, 1946)
DOCUMENT NO. 16
THE MINISTER IN HUNGARY (SCHOENFELD) TO THE SECRETARY OF STATE*

SECRET   BUDAPEST, April 20, 1946—9 p.m.
URGENT   [Received April 22—3:20 p.m.]

742. Mytel 737, April 19.[75] PriMin asked me to call and told me today that during his visit at Moscow he had spent altogether nearly 8 hours on two occasions with Stalin. He had explained to Russians he felt it was necessary to take positive steps to end isolation of Hungary and to establish personal contact with Sov Govt as he hoped to do later with other great powers.

PriMin said he had then raised political issue by indicating Hungarian policy was directed first to cooperation with great powers in establishing durable peace, secondly, to safeguarding development of Hungarian democracy and thirdly to protection of interests of large number of Hungarians outside borders of Hungary. To these ends settlement with Czecho and Rumania was necessary. Referring to Czecho, he had pointed out that desire of Benes to expel all Hungarians from Czecho meant further impoverishment for Hungary where density of population, as Gyöngyösi has often said to me, is already excessive for agricultural country. Moreover he had argued Hungarians in Slovakia were settled closely packed along border with Hungary. If these Hungarians were deprived of "equal rights" in Czecho and also of minority rights, Hungary

---

*FRUS, 1946, 6, pp. 280–83

should in all justice receive the territory where this dense population has so long been settled. Molotov and Stalin had pointed out
this was matter for decision by Allied Powers and made no territorial commitment but agreed Hungarians in Czecho were entitled to
equal rights.

On Transylvania question, PriMin said he had pointed out that
since more than one million Hungarians in Transylvania lived deep
in Rumanian territory, Hungary did not aspire to territory in that
particular area. However, there were approximately one-half million Hungarians adjacent to present frontier. Nearly one million
Rumanians also live in this adjacent area and Hungary would be
willing to incorporate them with full rights subject to determination by the powers whether these Rumanians should be mutually
exchanged for about same number Hungarians living in the more
remote settled region of Transylvania. Molotov and Stalin heard
this Hungarian proposal without raising objection but Stalin mentioned that language of Rumanian armistice re right of Rumania to
acquire all of [or] greater part of Transylvania suggested Hungary
had basis for claim of some territorial adjustment. Russians however emphasized this was matter for decision by armistice signa-
tories. PriMin said these statements by Stalin must be considered
strictly secret.

PriMin expressed confidence positive results had been achieved
during Moscow visit and his strong conviction that he now had free
hand to manage his Govt. He had not been called upon for slightest
political undertakings. He said it was his hope to establish same
relations of confidence with other Allied Powers and perhaps to
make similar visits to their capitals as opportunity offered but he
felt we would understand it was his first duty to establish personal
relations with Soviet leaders.

Sent Dept; repeated to London as No. 194; Paris for Dunn US
No. 89 and Moscow as No. 172.

SCHOENFELD

THE FOREIGN SERVICE
OF THE UNITED STATES
OF AMERICA*

DOCUMENT NO. 17

S E C R E T   AMERICAN LEGATION
                                        Budapest, Hungary, April 22, 1946.

Dear Jimmie:

Supplementing my telegrams reporting conversations with the Hungarian Prime Minister and Foreign Minister, respectively, and giving the gist of other available information regarding the course of the conversations between members of the Hungarian Delegation who recently visited Moscow and representatives of the Soviet Government, including Stalin and Molotov, I now enclose for your secret information a translation of Notes which I understand were kept by Dr. Gyongyosi, the Hungarian Foreign Minister, of conversations on April 9, 11, and 12, respectively, in which Gyongyosi participated. This information reaches me in a manner which I consider entirely reliable and the translation enclosed is, I believe, to be depended on as accurate.

The enclosed Notes confirm the substance of my telegrams but also contain some additional facts and color which, I think, should be very helpful to you in your negotiations affecting the Hungarian and Rumanian Treaties.

Although the visit of the Hungarian Delegation lasted from April 9, to April 18, only the three days mentioned are covered by the enclosed Notes.

With best wishes for the success of your work and warm personal regards, I am, as ever,

                                        Very sincerely yours,

                                        H. F. Arthur Schoenfeld
                                        American Minister

----

*Box 100, RG-43, N.A.

The Honorable
 James C. Dunn,
 American Deputy to the
 Council of Foreign Ministers
 Paris, France.

Enclosure:
 Translation of Notes
 dated April 9, 11, and 12, 1946.

TRANSLATION OF NOTES KEPT BY THE HUNGARIAN FOREIGN MINISTER REGARDING CONVERSATIONS WITH SOVIET REPRESENTATIVES DURING THE VISIT TO MOSCOW OF THE HUNGARIAN PRIME MINISTER

April 9, 1945-April 18, 1946, Inclusive

April 9, 1946.

Molotov received us at 6:30 p.m. He was with Dekanozov, Deputy Foreign Minister, Pushkin and his secretary Pavlov, Hungarians: myself, Minister Szekfu and Secretary Niszkacs as interpreter.

Upon Molotov's request I outlined to him my ideas about territorial questions connected with the preparation of peace. Hungary has territorial problems with only two countries: Czechoslovakia and Roumania. As regards Czechoslovakia, the question was not raised by us. It was forced on us as a consequence of the first Prague discussion, when they insisted on transferring from Slovakia a large amount of Hungarians to Hungary. To show our friendliness we accepted the principle of exchange of population. According to Masaryk's estimate the number of Slovaks accepting voluntary transfer to Slovakia was about 2-300.000. On the basis of present information, their number does not exceed 50-60.000, so that after the exchange of population about 600.000 Hungarians would remain in Slovakia. The Czechs plan to grant Czechoslovak citizenship to about 200.000/either because they speak the language or because they have Slovak relatives or ancestors/. In view of the bad conditions in which the Hungarians live in Slovakia it is possible that many will take Slovakian citizenship. The balance of 400,000 would be divided as follows: about half would be distributed in Czechoslovakia and the other half transferred to Hungary. This would be too heavy a load on Hungary and we therefore ask for assistance in trying to obtain that the Hungarians remain in Czechoslovakia without being disturbed and with equal civil rights.

If, however, the Czechs should insist on the transfer of Hungarians, the territorial question becomes acute.

Molotov listened with attention. He expressed his approval on our having made an agreement on exchange of population and his hope that the Czechoslovaks will grant equal rights to Hungarians in Slovakia.

I then submitted the Transylvanian question and the two proposals which we have worked out to settle the Roumanian Border. The first proposal includes annexation to Hungary of 11.800 square Km with 967.000 inhabitants, of which 442.000 are Hungarian and 421.000 Roumanian, while 104.000 of other nationality/German and Slovak/. This would be the ethnical rearrangement of the boundary, which has the disadvantage of leaving the larger part of Hungarians in Roumania, while many Roumanians would remain on Hungarian territory. The sound public opinion is not so much worried by the territorial question as by the destiny of Hungarians which will be left on Roumanian territory. We know that Groza's policy has been friendly to the Hungarians, but we also know that his policy is sabotaged by his officials and by the reactionaries.

Molotov asked which were the main complaints on the part of Hungarians in Roumania.

I replied that the complaints are particularly of an economic character. Every effort is made to destroy Hungarians economically. This does not affect only middle class and the wealthier class, which is easier to understand, but also the small farmer and poor people, workers, small traders, etc. Not even fanatics believe in Hungary that it is possible to obtain the territory where the Szekely population lives. Our plan is therefore to have as many Roumanians on Hungarian territory as Hungarians on Roumanian territory. This is the basis of the second plan which applies to a territory of 22.000 Km^2. This is not more than one fifth of Transylvania. This territory includes 900.000 Roumanians so that there still would be 180.000 Hungarians in excess on Roumanian territory, i.e. 1.080.000. But generally speaking it would result in an approximate equilibrium, which is the best guarantee for the two countries treating their minorities humanly. If however this treatment could not be secured, the second plan offers the advantage of making possible an exchange of population and all Hungarians or Roumanians could be settled down on this territory of 22.000 Km^2. This territory also has a certain economic basis and a geographic justification. It includes forests which are important to Hungary, a considerable production of sulphur/for fertilizers/a small production of metals. The loss would not affect Roumania sensibly.

Molotov listened with attention and said that in the Armistice agreement the Allies had promised to assist Roumania in the reannexation of Transylvania or of the larger part of Transylvania.

I replied that our plan was not in contradiction to this as our maximum demand is 22.000 Km^2 i.e. $1/5$ of the whole Transylvanian territory.

Molotov thanked me and without giving me a hint as to the Soviet intentions, the conversation was terminated.

April 11

Stalin received us at the Kremlin at 9:30 p.m. Hungarians: myself, Nagy Ferenc, Szakasits, Geroe and Szekfue. Russians: Stalin, Molotov, Dekanozov, Puskin and Grigoriev, as interpreter.

Nagy Ferenc: He thanked Stalin for liberation and for the democratic development which the country could obtain through Russian assistance. He talked about land reform, nationalization of mines, supervision of banks. He said that he thought it necessary to report on the results of one year of Hungarian democracy. Stalin interrupted him and said that Hungary is a free and independent country and therefore her Prime Minister is not obliged to make reports, so that he considers Nagy's expose as the communication of a friendly country. Nagy then spoke about the fight against reaction. Stalin then spoke about the difficult economic situation of Hungary, particularly about inflation. The Prime Minister outlined the recent economic program of the Hungarian Government. He requested Stalin to send one or two Soviet economic experts to Hungary to help the Hungarian Government with their advice by examining the economic situation and finding a solution of difficulties.

Stalin asked about the behaviour of the Red Army in Hungary. The Prime Minister said that there has been some trouble in the past, as it always happens in the case of occupation, but that complaints were now reduced to a minimum. Stalin then said that the occupying troops would be soon withdrawn from Hungary and only small detachments would remain.

Then, the matter of reparations was discussed. The Prime Minister said that reparations represent a great difficulty to Hungary, under present economic conditions. The Government intends to do his best to comply with obligations, but they do not know whether this will be possible. He asked for extension of the reparation period. Stalin said he agrees and details will have to be discussed.

Nagy then mentioned Red Army claims for payment of railroad expenses. Stalin was much amused by Gero's expose. The Red Army asked for payment of 14 million dollars for work which was largely done by Hungarian workers. When Gero said that claims include repairs done on lines which are located in Austria and Czechoslovakia, Stalin burst out laughing. He told Gero not to pay.

Gero then said that the Red Army has painted Russian trophies on MAV cars, which are then leased to the Hungarian Railways at very high international rates. Stalin said that in his opinion the cars which were owned by Hungary and which are required for transportation by the Hungarian railways should be returned to the Hungarian railways.

Nagy asked for the assistance of the Soviet Union and of the Generalissimo in the question of Hungarian displaced property in the Western European territory. Stalin said that Hungary will have these assets returned, at least the gold.

Nagy then mentioned peace preparation. He said that we have no claims towards Yugoslavia. He then mentioned Czechoslovakia on the same lines as outlined by me to Molotov on April 9. Stalin said it would be necessary for the two countries to make an agreement including an exchange of population. Nagy then said that there are many more Hungarians in Slovakia then vice versa. Stalin said this is not the substance of the problem, the Soviets have transferred 1 million Poles and obtained only 100,000 Ukrainians and in spite of this the Soviets have realized the exchange of population. However, not all Governments are able to take such courageous measures.

Then I commented on the subject in the same manner as in the case of Molotov.

Stalin replied that the Czechs would be willing to discuss territorial questions, but they are afraid of the Slovaks. Stalin said that in his opinion the obtaining of equal rights for Hungarians in Slovakia is absolutely justified.

Nagy then spoke about the Transylvanian question and that the Foreign Minister had certain plans on this subject. Puskin interrupted and said that the Foreign Minister has maps. Thereupon I showed the maps to Stalin who rose from his seat and looked at the map with great interest. I outlined my plans as already done to Molotov. During the whole time, Stalin listened attentively and looked several times at the map. He asked twice whether any exchange of population was involved in the plan, whereupon I said that it was not included in the plan but that it was possible under the plan. Stalin joked and said that if the Soviets accept the plan, the King of Roumania will abdicate. Nagy said that Roumania would then at least become a Republic like Hungary. Stalin then asked Molotov about the terms of the Roumanian Armistice Agreement. Molotov told him that the Allies will support the Roumanian claims for all or at least the greater part of Transylvania. Stalin thought a while and then said that he would think the matter over and that we will meet again.

The interview lasted two hours.

The whole conversation had the character of a friendly talk under the influence of Stalin's personality, which though giving the impression of his historic individuality, also showed his human and encouraging side. The delegation was at first somewhat embarrassed, because at the beginning Stalin looked rather stern. But then we saw that his severity was due more to the interest he was taking in the matter and to concentration of his attention. He showed sparks of the Stalin humor and this encouraged the members of the delegation, who felt that it stood in front of the greatest son of a great country and of the perhaps greatest popular personality of history whose monumentality did not however lack a certain community of spirit with us.

April 12

At 6:30 a two hours interview at the Foreign Office with Dekanozov and Grigorjev, the latter acting as interpreter.

The first question raised by me was the problem of war prisoners. I asked for permission of correspondence to be granted to PWs. D. agreed and said that details should be discussed. I suggested that correspondence should be made possible on cards printed in Russian (difficulties are mainly due to the fact that the Russians have not a sufficient number of censors speaking Hungarian). In addition of securing by this method news to the families, it would also give us an idea of how many prisoners there still are. I asked D. to authorize Szekfue to discuss details with the Soviet Foreign Office.

D. agreed to my request. I also asked for authorization to have the Soviet Foreign Office forward the 200 letters sent by PW family members to the Hungarian Legation in Moscow D. Agreed. I also asked him to make it possible for PWs, who have special political merits to return home exceptionally. D. Agreed to this also.

I then mentioned the 1 million Rubel loan to be given to our Legation. Puskin had told me in Budapest that the matter would be arranged as soon as the Legation was established. Up to now only 100,000 rubels were received. This causes difficulties. D. told me he knew about the matter. His financial advisers told him that it was necessary first to make an agreement. He advised me to discuss the matter with Mr. Csucsulin at the Vnyestorg bank. I also told him that the National Bank had transferred money and that the Legation had not received any notice. D. said he did not know this matter.

I then outlined our peace plans. The matter is not only important but also very urgent, due to the meeting of the Foreign Ministers on April 25. In this situation it was my aim to try and find out what the Soviet intentions are in respect to South Eastern Europe. I do not want the Soviets to inform me of their views as I suppose that this is not possible. My intention is to ascertain whether our plans are not in opposition to Soviet political interests. My policy was from the beginning friendly to the Soviets and I do not want to make plans which would be contrary to Soviet political interests. D. agreed to what I said and I then spoke about Czechoslovakia and told him how glad and thankful we were that Stalin had approved of our contention as regards equal rights to Hungarians in Slovakia. Stalin's assistance in this matter is of great value to us and fills us with hope. I then outlined the Roumanian program in the same manner as to Molotov. I understand—I said—that Soviet Union is friendly both to Roumania and to Hungary and does not wish to affect the interests of either of these countries. Therefore I do not insist on having a decided support. But I would like to know if the smaller plan is not in contrast with Soviet plans.

D. said he understands our difficulties and also personally my difficulties in trying to satisfy the demands of my party. What claims will be made at the Peace conference is a matter to be decided by the Hungarian Government, particularly by Nagy Ferenc, as Prime Minister and leader of the majority party. In his opinion, the Prime Minister should discuss the matter with Groza, attempting to reach an agreement with him.

I then asked D. whether the Soviet Union would give active support for such an agreement to be reached.

D. then said they cannot do it for political reasons. This is the task of the two Prime Ministers.

I then said that if the Soviets do not participate intensively in such agreement to be reached, I do not see any possibility of concluding an agreement. I had suggested an exchange of views with Groza to Puskin in writing, but have received no answer. Anyhow it is too late now, as we have only two weeks before the beginning of the Peace Conference.

D. agreed that the time was too short.

I added that in any case I did not see any possibility to reach an agreement. If Groza renounces one square kilometer of territory before elections, he would cause himself great damage politically. The Hungarian Government would be accused of having lost a possibility of obtaining a much better result, if it had not yielded in the discussions with Groza. Responsibility is so large that neither of the two Governments can undertake it. Already in the case of the Czechoslovak negotiations we agreed with Clementis that regardless of the goodwill of both of us in the cardinal questions, the political problems involved are such that they can be solved only by an international decision.

I told D. that my idea was to submit to the Peace Conference our maximum demand, as Groza will evidently also submit his maximum demand of the whole Transylvanian territories. Both Tatarescu and Groza have declared publicly that they consider the present boundaries as definitive. In my opinion Groza would suffer no harm if we submit the maximum proposal. If we submitted a proposition which would be accepted immediately by the Allies, it might mean a defeat for Groza, but if we come with a proposition and in this connection Groza obtains a certain success this position is even better. If we see that the maximum demand does not meet the understanding of the Allies, we have still the smaller plan as a reserve.

D. only said that the Roumanian Armistice Agreement applies to the annexation to Roumania of Transylvania or of a large part of Transylvania. I then said that our maximum demand did not represent more than one fifth of Transylvania. D. did not make any comment to this.

In the long and lively interview I was unable to ascertain the Soviet opinion on the matter D. then asked whether the Hungarian Delegation at the Peace Conference was already appointed. I told him that there was a plan under which the delegation would be composed of the Foreign Minister, the representatives of the parties and the experts but that this plan had not yet been finally discussed.

THE FOREIGN SERVICE OF THE UNITED STATES OF AMERICA* DOCUMENT NO. 18

S E C R E T   AMERICAN LEGATION
Budapest, Hungary, April 23, 1946.

Dear Jimmie:

Supplementing my letter of yesterday, I now enclose transla-tion of Notes by the Hungarian Foreign Minister, Dr. Gyongyosi, of a conversation on April 15, 1946 at Moscow between members of the Hungarian Delegation and Foreign Minister Molotov.

I also enclose translation of excerpts from the toast delivered by Stalin at a dinner for the Hungarian Delegation on April 16, 1946.

I enclose two extra copies of these two papers and would ask you to be so kind as to turn them over to Mr. Reber for the Department's files. I sent him duplicate copies of my letter of April 22, 1946 to you before I knew he would be with you in Paris, as I gather from today's radio bulletin.

With best regards, I am,

Very sincerely yours,

H. F. Arthur Schoenfeld
American Minister

Enclosures: (2) (In triplicate)
  1. Translation of Notes by Hungarian Foreign Minister dated April 15, 1946.
  2. Translation of excerpts from toast delivered by Stalin on April 16, 1946.

The Honorable
   James C. Dunn,
   American Deputy to the
   Council of Foreign Ministers,
   Paris, France.

---

*Box 100, RG-43, N.A.

TRANSLATION OF NOTES KEPT BY THE HUNGARIAN FOREIGN MINISTER REGARDING CONVERSATIONS WITH SOVIET REPRESENTATIVES DURING THE VISIT TO MOSCOW OF THE HUNGARIAN PRIME MINISTER

April 15, 1946.

April 15.

Prime Minister, Foreign Minister, Molotov, Pushkin, Kemeny Secretary of Legation, Grigorjev Secr. of Legation

Molotov, replying to the questions raised in Moscow by the Hungarian Delegation, first spoke about the Czechoslovak and Roumanian problems. In his opinion these questions should be settled by negotiations directly with the countries concerned. In connection with Roumania he emphasized the fact that it would not be advisable to submit the question to the Peace Conference, without having it first discussed with Roumania.

Gyongyosi said—after the Prime Minister stated that Hungary agrees with Molotov's suggestion and will attempt to realize it—that the plan involves difficulties. He indicated that both CSR and Roumania will have elections soon and their governments would have difficulties with public opinion if they agreed prior to elections with any proposal which might be unpopular. This circumstance also affected the Prague negotiations, as although the negotiators could have agreed on many points, they were handicapped by politics. This is indicated also by the protocol of the Prague negotiations by the sentence that any problems which cannot be solved through negotiations will be submitted internationally. Hungary has already had elections but the public opinion represented by the majority party is just as difficult to handle as in Roumania. If direct negotiations do not lead to a positive result, the Government will be accused of having made an error and that it would have been better to submit the question to the Peace Conference. Therefore, Hungary is able to negotiate the matter directly only if the Soviet Union is ready to initiate these discussions.

The Prime Minister interrupted and said that he believes it is desirable to have a mutual agreement between the two interested countries and in his opinion, if the countries do not agree, they must be made to agree.

Gyongyosi then asked in connection with Roumania which of the two countries should propose to start negotiations. Molotov said that it was only natural that the proposition should come from the country which has more interest in the matter, in this case Hungary. Gyongyosi then asked whether the Soviet Union would approve of such an initiative. Molotov gave an affirmative answer.

The Prime Minister then said that all South Eastern democracies have troubles and that Hungary understands the difficult position of the Groza government and that it is in Hungary's interest to have Groza remain on his post. However, it is natural that Hungary is most interested in her own troubles. Molotov smiled in a manner which looked understanding.

Gyongyosi said that according to press news, the Roumanian delegation had already been invited to the conference and it has arrived in Paris, accompanied by a substantial documentation. Molotov said this was just a sensational report on the part of correspondents and that Hungary will be also invited and that Roumania will not be in a more favorable situation than Roumania at the Peace Conference (*sic*). Prime Minister said he had read that the Roumanians had taken to Paris two carloads of documents. Molotov said smiling that it is not the quantity of documents which will influence decisions in Paris. Prime Minister said that at the Peace Conference they will not even read 2 kilos of documents and that if decisions could be affected by the weight of underlying documents, Hungary would have difficulties due to her shortage in transportation.

On reparations, Molotov said that the Soviet Union agrees to extend the term of 6 years to 8 years. The term for the wool and cotton processing shall also be extended until the middle of next year. He is willing to permit returning home of sick PWs and correspondence with their families will also be permitted. Details will have to be discussed separately.

As regards railroad transportation problems, these shall be discussed by the competent ministries of the two countries.

Thanking for the concessions made by the Soviet Union as regards the question of PWs, the Prime Minister said that he would like to raise a concrete question in this connection. Molotov interrupted and said that the delegation would have another opportunity to see Stalin and on this occasion they may mention any further question which has not been discussed heretofore. The Prime Minister thanked him and said that the Red Army have made prisoners many people, who were not members of fighting units and who were not even soldiers. This is not a large percentage of the Hungarian PWs, they do not exceed 10.000, but as many are farmers and they are required for cultivation in spring, the Hungarian Government would like them to be released exceptionally.

Molotov said he had not heard of this before and he wants to obtain information but in principle he is in favor of the proposed solution, which must however first be discussed.

Pushkin interrupted and said that this matter had been mentioned in Budapest, he had asked for lists but the Legation has never received these lists.

Gyongyosi said that these lists were progressively forwarded to the Legation. Molotov interrupted and said that he would do his best to obtain a favorable solution of the matter.

Then Molotov said that the communique should be worded in common and that it should contain only generalities although satisfying Hungarian and Soviet public opinion. Then, technical details regarding the communique were discussed, especially as regards inclusion of the concession on the reparation term.

The Prime Minister thanked Molotov for Hungary having been able to obtain an important success on all matters dependent on the decision of the Soviet Union.

TRANSLATION OF EXCERPTS FROM THE TOAST DELIVERED BY STALIN AT A DINNER FOR THE HUNGARIAN DELEGATION ON APRIL 16, 1946

At present it seems that many medium and small countries are afraid of the Soviets. This fear is unjustified. Lenin stated that all nations, large or small, have their particular value and importance from the point of view of humanity. This principle still rules in Soviet policy. More than half of the Soviet population is non Russian, and consists of many nationalities. These nationalities enjoy complete autonomy and freedom.

The Soviets have always had sympathy for Hungary and always wanted to be on friendly terms with her. This was true even when the Hungarian regime was not democratic. Stalin then spoke about the Hungarian flags of 1849 which had been returned to Hungary by the Soviets in 1941. At that time, declarations made by Hungarians induced the Soviet to believe that Hungary was a real friend. In their simplicity the Soviet leaders did not know that this was only a fake. A few months after the flags had been returned, Hungary declared war on Russia. The fight was long and bloody. Horthy later was prepared to make an Armistice, but he had no character and energy. Szalasi continued the fight. Under such circumstances the Red Army could do nothing else than to fight too.

The Russian people have a debt towards Hungary. The Armies of the Czar helped the Austrians in 1849 to defeat the revolutionary Hungarian army. However, the Soviet Union, who executed the last Czar, Nicholas II, is not responsible for the sins of the Czarist regime.

He is now glad to know that the leaders of the Hungarian Nation are democrats and that they have come to Moscow. He emphasizes the fact that the Soviet Union always wanted friendship with Hungary, regardless of the latter's Government.

He then emptied his glass to the health of the friendly relations between Russia and Hungary.

BUDAPEST* ~~DOCUMENT NO. 19~~   April 25, 5 pm 1946
    SECRET   100
Secret   April 27, 4 am

From reliable source it is learned that at Foreign Affairs Committee of Assembly yesterday Gyongyosi stated Soviets had approved return of part of Transylvania to Hungary. At meeting with British MPs today Gyongyosi asked them to support this Hungarian claim. In reply they inquired what Great Britain could expect in return to which Gyongyosi could not provide satisfactory answer. . . .

                                                    Schoenfeld

---

*Box 96, RG-43, N.A.

C.
Hungarian-Czechoslovak Conflict and the Paris Conference

DOCUMENT NO. 20

25 Août 1945

Télégramme en clair par courrier*
DIPLOFRANCE PARIS No. 77

Je réponds à votre télégramme No. 97.

Je vous communique par dépêche le résumé des renseignements recueillis sur les expulsions d'Allemands et de Hongrois.

A—*Sudètes.* Au cours d'un entretien avec M. Clementis qui continue à diriger les Affaires Etrangères en l'absence de M. Masaryk, le S/Secrétaire d'Etat m'a déclaré que le Gouvernement tchécoslovaque s'en tiendrait strictement aux décisions de la Conférence de Potsdam et ne procédera à aucune expulsion sans l'assentiment préalable de la Commission Interalliée de Berlin. . . .

B—*Hongrois.* Ainsi que l'a indiqué M. Clementis la question de l'expulsion des Hongrois diffère de celle de l'expulsion des Allemands. Il s'agit là d'abord plutôt d'un échange que d'un transfert de populations, les Slovaques de Hongrie devant être rapatriés au moment même où les Hongrois seront expulsés de Tchécoslovaquie.

D'autre part, l'organisation du transfert des Hongrois ne dépend pas du bon vouloir des Trois grandes puissances, mais seulement de l'approbation des autorités militaires russes, seules responsables de l'ordre en Hongrie.

---

*MAE, Série Y, Carton 45, Dossier 6.

Aussi le Gouvernement Tchécoslovaque va-t-il pouvoir envoyer très prochainement à Budapest une mission analogue à celle qu'il désirerait envoyer à Berlin. Les conditions matérielles du transport seront aisément précisées avec les commissions soviétiques. Et, dès que l'accord soviétique sera acquis, le Gouvernement de Prague traitera directement avec le Gouvernement de Budapest pour déterminer les dates et lieux des transferts, et la destination sur laquelle chaque groupe devra être dirigé.

M. Clementis se propose à cette occasion d'aller lui-même à Budapest et de régler la question du transfert des Hongrois dans le cadre général d'un accord de bon voisinage. J'ai cru comprendre que le S/Secrétaire d'Etat aux Affaires Etrangères envisagerait de soulever la question de la rectification de la frontière slovaque.

M. Clementis m'a rappelé qu'il m'avait demandé dès le mois de Juin dernier, & plusieurs fois depuis lors, quelle solution la France entendait donner au problème des transferts d'Allemands et si elle adhérerait sans réserve aux décisions prises à Potsdam. Tout en indiquant qu'absents de Potsdam, nous n'avons pas encore les données nécéssaires pour prendre position, j'ai répondu à M. Clementis que je ferais part à Votre Excellence du souci du Gouvernement tchécoslovaque d'être informé directement de la position que nous entendons prendre./.

Keller

THE AMBASSADOR IN CZECHOSLOVAKIA (STEINHARDT) TO THE SECRETARY OF STATE* DOCUMENT NO. 21

SECRET   PRAHA, May 7, 1946—midnight.
                                          [Received May 8—5:20 p.m.]

727. For the Secretary and Riddleberger. President Beneš asked me to call to see him this morning. He said he was becoming increasingly concerned at the insistence of the Hungarian Govt on creating what he described as a state within a state by seeking minority rights for the Hungarians residing in Czechoslovakia. He pointed out that the prewar German and Hungarian minorities in Czechoslovakia had opened the gates to the Nazis in 1938 and 1939 and expressed the opinion that as the German minority was being transferred to Germany under the Potsdam decision, the Hungarian minority should likewise be transferred to Hungary. He argued that as Hungary was transferring its German minority to Germany, the Hungarian minority from Czechoslovakia should take the place of these individuals and that, therefore, the claim of the Hungarian Govt that there would be no space available to receive its minority from Czechoslovakia was not made in good faith, but was advanced solely for the purpose of maintaining a Hungarian bridgehead in Czechoslovakia. He indicated on the map that a Hungarian bridgehead in Slovakia might be as dangerous at some time in the future as was the German bridgehead in Bohemia at the outbreak of the last war.

Beneš then stated that in the course of the talks between the Czechoslovak representatives in Paris and Molotov, when the former had stressed the desire of the Czechoslovak Govt to transfer its Hungarian minority to Hungary, Molotov had indicated his acquiescence but had added "I must first find out how the Americans feel about it as without the Americans I can do nothing." Beneš added with obvious relish that he had repeated Molotov's remark at a Cabinet meeting yesterday for the benefit of the Communist members of the Govt who had been visibly "shocked" to learn that the Soviet Govt did not regard itself as omnipotent.

---

*FRUS, 1946, 6, pp. 368–69. Cf. Box 96, RG-43, N.A.

At the close of his remarks Beneš referred to the fact that the Soviets had "received all of the credit" in Czechoslovakia for the Potsdam decision authorizing the transfer of the German minority to Germany and expressed the hope that if a favorable decision is arrived at in Paris authorizing the transfer of the Hungarian minority to Hungary, the decision would be conveyed to him immediately "so that this time the US will at least share in the credit."

Sent Paris 107, repeated Dept 727.

Steinhardt

Budapest* **DOCUMENT NO. 22**   August 9, 2 p.m.
312
SECRET   August 10

Following is substance of July 31 report from Szekfu Hungarian Minister Moscow to FONMIN Budapest detailing interview with Dekanozov re Soviet position with respect Zecho claims Hungary:

Dekanozov interpreted communique issued conclusion Zecho Soviet talks as meaning Soviet support in Paris for just desires Czechs. Expulsion two hundred thousand Hungarians considered by Soviets in this category. Dekanozov did not know if figure quoted includes 70 to 80 thousand Magyars involved in Czech Hungarian population exchange agreement. He emphasized 2 hundred thousand as maximum figure and assured Szekfu remaining Hungarians Zech would have full rights in accord Soviet policy protecting minorities.

Dekanozov declared Soviets will adhere draft Hungarian treaty awarding all Transylvania to Rumania but that in accord Soviet principles re minorities rights Hungarian minority Transylvania will be defended. Equality guarantees in draft Hungarian Treaty for racial religious linguistic minorities in Rumania explained on this basis. Szekfu inclined to doubt Soviet support in Paris on question 2 to 3 hundred thousand Hungarians who left and then returned Transylvania if this question raised by Hungarian Delegation.

Dekanozov gave no committal reply on question Soviet support Zecho claim to Bratislava bridgehead but Szekfus impression was Soviets will support this claim in view Dekanozov's rejection Szekfus presentation Hungarian arguments this matter. Sent Dept; repeated Paris for SECDEL 312, Moscow 266. Dept please pass to Moscow (Dekanozov also stated he had prepared draft Hungarian Treaty and took credit for certain concessions economic clauses. Szekfu replied it would be regrettable if fulfillment Zecho demands made final text more burdensome than draft. Szekfu regarded entire conversation as confirmation view that Czechs have completely won Soviet support for their claims against Hungarian and

---

*Box 96, RG-43, N.A.

concluded that neither historical nor emotional arguments nor appeals to fairness influence Soviets. He suggested keying Hungarian arguments more in direction Soviet ideological considerations.

Translation of text follows by despatch.

Schoenfeld

S-6

POLITICAL AND TERRITORIAL COMMISSION FOR HUNGARY*

Chairman:	Yugoslavia—Sinisa Stankovic
Vice Chairman:	Australia—A. T. Stirling
Rapporteur:	Ukraine—Mr. Ptoukha
Members:	United States of America
	Australia
	Byelorussia
	Canada
	France
	Great Britain
	India

DOCUMENT NO. 23

	New Zealand
	Czechoslovakia
	Ukraine
	U.S.S.R.
	Union of South Africa
	Yugoslavia

Secretary:	Mr. Burin des Roziers
Associate Secretary:	Mr. Richard Sears, Jr.
Assistant Secretaries:	Mr. Devilleneuve
	Miss Merkling

U.S. Participants:

Ambassador Walter Bedell Smith
James C. H. Bonbright
Frederick T. Merrill (recording)

Subcommittee

Chairman:	Ukraine—Mr. Ptoukha
Vice Chairman:	None
Rapporteur:	New Zealand—P. Costello
Members:	Canada Czechoslovakia
	New Zealand Ukraine
Secretary:	Mr. Burin des Roziers

Attending for Secretary General of Conference: Richard Sears

U.S. Participants:	None

FRUS, 1946, IV, p. 872.

SEVENTEENTH PLENARY MEETING, AUGUST 14, 1946, 4 P.M.*

Verbatim Record

DOCUMENT NO. 24

President: Mr. Byrnes (U.S.A.)

THE PRESIDENT: (Interpretation): The meeting is opened. . . .

THE PRESIDENT: The Conference will now hear the statement of the Hungarian Delegation as was decided previously.

I request the Secretary-General to introduce the Hungarian Delegation.

(The Hungarian Delegation was introduced into the Conference by the Secretary-General).

THE PRESIDENT: (Interpretation): In the name of the Conference I welcome the Hungarian Delegation. Their views will be put forward by the Hungarian Minister of Foreign Affairs and I now request him to speak.

[MR. GYÖNGYÖSI:] Mr. President, Fellow Delegates—Allow me to begin by expressing my gratitude for the invitation you sent to Hungary to appear at this Conference, thus enabling the Hungarian Government to state its views on the peace treaty which will mark the end of the second world war.

The fact of being allowed to appear and to speak freely fills us with the hope that, this time, the peace negotiations will be different from those we knew over twenty-five years ago. We hope that the settlement resulting from the present talks, will establish a lasting peace, that will assure to the Danubian States a healthy development; this will contribute to a large extent, to ensure the pacification of the whole of Europe, and the rest of the world; it was from Eastern Europe that the sparks burst which twice set the world on fire, provoking the world wars which brought endless sufferings to mankind.

One of the most important guarantees of a lasting settlement is the fact that, contrary to the happenings of 1919, it is being elaborated with the aid and approval of the Soviet Union and the U.S.A.

---

*FRUS, 1946, 3, pp. 210–21.

Representing a vanquished nation, but full of apprehension and fear for the future of mankind, I would like, first, to make two remarks. A peace treaty marks the end of a war. It has necessarily grave consequences for the vanquished. But a peace treaty is at the same time the basis for the future, it is a new beginning, an instrument to eliminate the causes of friction and to ensure the reconstruction of the devastated countries, the reinstatement of distressed populations and the restoration of broken international relations. A peace treaty is thus a sharp division between the past and the future. In our common interest, a peace treaty should take into account the liquidation of past errors and the necessity of establishing a better future. The repressive clauses contained in a peace treaty should, then, be counterbalanced by constructive possibilities which it guarantees.

It is a new, a democratic Hungary that appears to-day before the Conference. The liberating forces of 1848 and the democratic energy of 1918 are united in her. To-day, as on those two occasions, the Hungarian people have taken their fate into their own hands; this time, they will retain it. In a diplomatic note recognising on behalf of the Soviet Government the Hungarian Government, Marshal Voroshilov noted the efforts made by the provisional Hungarian Government as having contributed to "the success of the struggle of the United Nations against Germany."

But apart from this first result, Hungarian democracy can show other positive results it has achieved in spite of extraordinary initial difficulties. An agrarian reform has completely ended feudal property, stern punishment has been meted out to the war-criminals of former regimes. Finally, first among all liberated countries, Hungary has held free elections by universal suffrage and secret ballot; she was first to institute a press free from all shackles, to re-establish the right to criticise freely and parliamentary institutions.

We know, of course, that the building of democracy cannot be the result of a few months' hasty work, we know there still, of necessity, persist some faults and failings; but the first results obtained are encouraging. If, to the contrary of what happened in 1918, the Hungarian democracy finds understanding and assistance; if the peace treaty assures to every Hungarian living in the Hungarian State or away from it, the possibility of living a free individual, social and national life, then the Hungarian Democracy will be able to face the future with confidence and will find it possible to take a useful and constructive part in the work of the democratic peoples.

As we are defending the future of Hungarian democracy, we do not want to forget or deny that in the great struggle just ended, through the fault of the reactionary regime, and social structure, as well as the blindness of its leaders, Hungary has sided against the cause which was that of all peoples and also of the Hungarian people. But the attitude of the Hungarian masses has hampered the actions of the Government; the events of March 1944, the occupation of the country by German troops, the repressions exercised by the German authorities, prove that, faced by the clear attitude of the Hungarian masses, the Hungarian leaders of the old regime could not serve the cause of National-Socialist Germany to the full measure Germany wished and certain States felt obliged to do. Moreover, the Hungarian peasants, the workers in the towns, the intellectuals have organised Resistance, have sabotaged the German War effort and many of them have contributed to the struggle for the liberation of other peoples. Up to the time Hungary was occupied by the Germans, a large number of persecuted people found there a refuge. This refuge was safeguarded there in spite of everything.

There cannot be any doubt that Hungary has fought this war at the side of Germany. It is in this that the responsibility is heavy. But this responsibility is different, both in quality and in quality [*quantity?*], from that falling on National-Socialism and Fascism, for the simple reason that, in a world conflict, a small nation sees its freedom of action severely limited. Whatever the measure of our responsibility it cannot implicate the whole of the Hungarian population, even if the debatable principle of collective security [*responsibility?*] is admitted.

Democratic Hungary repudiates aggressive, revisionist policy and true interpreter of the real feelings of the Hungarian nation, intends to live in peace and harmony with its neighbours. This in spite of the fact that after the first world war, one quarter of the Hungarian nation found itself, by virtue of the peace treaty, outside the frontiers of the Hungarian State. These Hungarians had the citizenship of the neighbouring States forced upon them, at a time when all nationalities tended to group themselves into States. The wish to see all Hungarians re-united into the frontiers of one national State should seem legitimate.

Nevertheless, it appears that the realisation of this aim is rendered difficult by geographical and political obstacles, not easily solved. That is why, the constantly acute problem consists—as the frontiers cannot be altered—in modifying the importance of the frontiers and in assuring to the Hungarians, living on the territory of another State, liberties that are the essential conditions of democracy, i.e. the right to live independently, free of want and fear, maintaining their national character.

Unfortunately, I am sorry to be compelled to observe that, very often, on [in] our regions, the condition of those belonging to a national minority, consists in being not only regarded as a national of another State, but being also deprived of the exercise of human rights and, partly, of the guarantee of human dignity.

The settlement which followed the first world war had clauses concerning territories peopled by minorities. These clauses have not always guaranteed the full respect of human rights, but, their application being controlled by the League of Nations, it was at least possible to have a right of appeal.

We are also aware that Hitlerite Germany has known, for its own Imperialist political needs, how to make full use of the guarantees assured to national minorities by the treaties. But the fact that she misused them does not justify the abandonment of a necessary guarantee. This is confirmed by the claims advanced by the international representatives of Jewish organisations, the most authoritative in the matter, as a result of the cruel persecutions they have endured.

It is known to the Hungarian Government that the United Nations Organisation intends to prepare a charter on human rights. This will take time. On the other hand, the United Nations Charter and the declarations of principle contained in the drafts of peace treaties, only mention certain liberties, leaving out the right of choosing one's domicile, the right of choosing one's language of instruction, the right of work and the right of enterprise. In a world torn by passions and national intolerance resulting from the war, it is precisely these liberties that it is essential to assure. It would then seem necessary, until the entry into force of the code to be issued by the United Nations Organisation, to come to an agreement whereby the States with a mixed central and Eastern European population, should pledge themselves to respect the exercise of these liberties. May I be allowed to refer in this matter to the memorandum handed to the Council of Foreign Ministers.

Events which occurred since the war produced in Hungary a feeling of uneasiness especially with regard to the position of the Hungarians in Roumania where there are more than a million and a half of them and in Czechoslovakia where, according to the Czechs' own statistics, there are more than six hundred and fifty thousand. The problem therefore concerns hundreds of thousands of individuals and relations between a number of States occupying an important part of Europe the lasting peace of which is involved.

Before I propose a solution of the problems concerning the Roumanian-Hungarian frontiers which we consider to be practicable, we must refer to a certain statement made here by the Head of the Roumanian Delegation. He seems to consider that the decision adopted by the four Foreign Ministers had settled the differences between Roumania and Hungary. For its own part, the Hungarian nation would not consider that this problem had been finally resolved. The Council of the Foreign Ministers abolished the Vienna Award, the work of Fascist Germany, and thereby automatically re-established the Roumanian frontier of 1938. But this in no way resolves the problem facing the two nations. It is true that the Head of the Roumanian Delegation was anxious to give assurances that his country would guarantee equal rights to her new Roumanian citizens. We note this declaration with satisfaction but, unfortunately, I am bound to state that the obviously excellent intentions of the Roumanian Government are frustrated by the chauvinistic spirit animating the authorities and by the anti-Hungarian feelings prevailing in the nationalist organisations. Anxiety is felt for the Hungarians not only in regard to the exercise by them of their political rights but mainly on account of the danger to which their status of equality in the economic plan is exposed with the consequent considerable impoverishment of the Hungarian population in Transylvania which is already apparent. We are glad to grasp the hand extended to us by the Roumanian Government because it is our long-felt desire to live in good understanding with our eastern neighbour. But we must first resolve the difference which undoubtedly exists between us. We suggested such a course spontaneously and on a number of occasions and proposed direct negotiations even before appealing to the Council of Foreign Ministers. We met with a refusal. We are even now prepared to accept any reasonable settlement involving the minimum of sacrifice to the two nations, a settlement which would lead to the establishment between us of conditions favouring a lasting peace and friendship.

We therefore request that the Conference should ask Roumania to send her delegates to confer with us. Let us try to settle these problems together. If these negotiations prove unsuccessful, the Conference could send a Commission with powers to investigate the situation on the spot and to draft a proposed solution for the consideration of the Conference.

Our standpoint is clear from the notes we have sent. We believed that we could understand the intentions of the great victorious powers from the armistice terms as signed by Roumania. Article 19 of these terms provided for the return of Transylvania, or at least of her major part to Roumania. We thought that on the basis of these terms we could make certain modest claims. We requested the return of only 22,000 of the 103,000 square kilometres of the Transylvania which lay within the boundaries of Hungary before the First World War. We did this in the hope that a solution of this kind would better serve the good understanding between the two nations. In practice this would mean that approximately the same number of Hungarians would remain within the boundaries of Roumania as there would be Roumanians on Hungarian territory. The two nations would, therefore, be equally interested in a satisfactory solution of the problem of minorities, with the result that wide territorial autonomies may be granted to them on both sides of the frontier.

In his speech from this rostrum, the Head of the Roumanian Delegation saw fit to claim reparations from Hungary.[*] We can discover no moral or legal justification for them. But I cannot dwell on the substance of this problem until the memorandum presented by the Roumanian Government on the subject of these claims is placed at the disposal of the Hungarian Government.

The other important problem which concerns the foreign policy of Hungary is that of its relations with Czechoslovakia. I wish to state that Democratic Hungary, which regards as its primary concern the good understanding and even the friendly co-operation with her neighbouring States looked most hopefully to Czechoslo-

---

[*]For text of Tatarescu's remarks, see the extract from the Verbatim Record of the 15th Plenary Meeting, August 13, p. 191.

kia. She saw her as the carrier of the noble ideas of Thomas Masaryk. Yet we were sadly disappointed when we discovered that, through no fault of ours, it became impossible to arrive at this good understanding. I therefore much regret that for this reason I must inform you of the difference which had appeared between Hungary and Czechoslovakia. While recovering from the chaos of war, Democratic Hungary was astonished and then grieved to witness the expulsion, in defiance of the rights of man, of thousands of Hungarians from Czechoslovakia, often at a few hours notice and only with a few items of hand-baggage. Six hundred and fifty thousand Hungarians living in Slovakia were deprived of their national status and of the most elementary human rights. Property belonging to citizens of Hungarian nationality was confiscated. No Hungarian may legally engage in any intellectual or manual labour. He may not appeal to a court or join a trade union or enjoy his rights as a citizen. The use of the Hungarian language is forbidden in public offices, often even in church and in any public place in general under threat of punishment. No periodical in the Hungarian language may appear in Czechoslovakia. Hungarian may not be spoken over the telephone, nor are telegrams in Hungarian accepted for transmission. No Hungarian may own a wireless set. There is no instruction carried out in Hungarian. Moreover, private tuition, if carried out in Hungarian, is punishable. The Czech authorities dismissed without compensation those officials employed by the State or in private business who were of Hungarian nationality. They stopped all payments of pensions and superannuation and war wounded, war widows and orphans no longer receive the subsistence allowances to which they were entitled.

Despite all these regrettable measures, the Hungarian Government did everything in its power to improve the relations between Hungary and Czechoslovakia. With this purpose in view but against its better sentiment the Hungarian Government thought it necessary to conclude, [through] negotiations between Hungary and Czechoslovakia, an agreement on the exchange of populations, as recommended by the great Powers. In accordance with the terms of this agreement, the Slovaks and Czechs who reside in Hungary may request to be transferred to Czechoslovakia. For its own part the Czechoslovak Government has the right to compulsory transfer to Hungary, of a number of Hungarians equal to that of the Slovaks and Czechs who had applied for permission to leave Hungary.

Under the provisions of this agreement, the Hungarian Government allowed a Czechoslovak Mission accompanied by a military escort, to devote six weeks to propaganda on Hungarian territory intended to induce the Slovaks to apply for a voluntary transfer. Seven hundred Czechoslovak agents were thus employed on Hungarian territory using every means of propaganda, making free use of Hungarian broadcasting facilities not to mention their press, proclamations and posters. In addition they organised public meetings, staged performances in the theatres and exhibited films.

As a result of this unprecedented propaganda, the number of Slovaks in Hungary to request their transfer amounted to one eighth, at the most, of the number of Hungarians in Czechoslovakia. Thus, even after this transfer, at least half a million Hungarians will still remain in Slovakia.

The Czechoslovak Government intends to push one portion of this considerable Hungarian population into Hungary, and to do away with the other portion by forcibly assimilating it. The Czechoslovak Government pretends to justify all these measures by arguing that the Hungarian minority had betrayed Czechoslovakia at the time of the Munich crisis. As to the attitude adopted by the Hungarian minority during that crisis, I venture to refer to a German secret document which was recently published by the U.S. Department of State. According to this document, on 16th September, Goering sent for the Hungarian Minister in Berlin and made representations to him on account of the indifferent attitude adopted by the Hungarians during the international crisis.

> The Hungarian press was keeping comparatively silent. In the Hungarian minority areas in Czechoslovakia it was completely calm in contrast to the situation in the Sudeten German areas.*

For our part, we shall stress and, if necessary, prove that the Hungarian minority played neither a decisive nor even an important part in the dismemberment of the Czechoslovak State in 1938. Indeed it constituted only a small percentage of the entire population. As in the case of the Slovenes, it only demanded a wider autonomy within the State. When an independent Slovakia was established

---

*For text of the German Foreign Office memorandum from which this excerpt is taken, see Department of State *Bulletin,* June 9, 1946, p. 984.

under German protection with the assent of a great majority of the Slovaks, the Hungarians of Slovakia alone refused to collaborate with the Germans and Slovaks and therefore suffered persecution. They openly declared against the establishment of Fascist rule and defended democracy and humane principles in parliament and in the press.

The forcible eviction of the Hungarians from Slovakia is not only morally and politically unjustifiable, it would confront Hungary with an economic, social and political problem which she is unable to solve. It must not be forgotten that the problem involves the eviction and resettlement of a rural population uprooted from their ancestral homes and land.

Gentlemen, however serious and desperate our position may be, the defeated party can never be denied the right of believing that such a demand is contrary to morality and humanity. And if a Hungarian Government could be found willing to accept it under outside pressure, it would be digging its own grave and the grave of Hungarian democracy by so doing. The land and the people who have tilled it for centuries and implanted their civilization therein, are indissolubly linked together. Such a bond could only be forcibly broken by violation of the fundamental laws of human existence. Czechoslovakia wants to keep territory inhabited by Hungarians. In that case let her keep the Hungarians also and give them the full rights of the individual and the citizen. If for any reason Czechoslovakia refuses to do so and insists on the forcible removal of the Hungarian minority, the Hungarian Government would be compelled to maintain the principle that the land is the people's.

The solution of the Hungarian-Czechoslovakian problem is hampered by the fact that essential differences emerge between the Hungarian and Czechoslovak standpoints on the facts just referred to. That is why the Hungarian Government feels it should ask the Peace Conference to send an international commission of experts to the spot who would enquire into all these questions and make the necessary investigations.

Turning to the economic problems, may I, Gentlemen, draw your attention to the risk that a peace treaty may reduce a country to permanent poverty. Democratic and peaceful development is, after all, hardly compatible with an economic situation which merely enables the population to live on the brink of starvation.

Preliminary study of the economic clauses of the draft treaty shows that they are even more burdensome than the corresponding clauses in the Armistice, which were already sufficiently severe. They maintain these clauses in principle, but aggravate them in detail, and there are a number of new clauses which augment the difficulties Hungary is already encountering and which threaten to impede the rehabilitation which is necessary for the execution of her international obligations. I am referring only to the articles providing for the liquidation of Hungarian property on United Nations territory and the recognition of any claims Hungary possess and those she may lodge against Germany and her ex-allies.

When it signed the Armistice, the Hungarian Government was still unable to form a true idea of the economic situation of the country. It was only when the common enemy had been driven out and the Government started on the work of reconstruction that it was able to form a better idea of the extent of the destruction.

It then became clear that the productive forces of the country and its national patrimony had been much more seriously damaged than was assumed at the time of the Armistice. The tasks involved in the work of reconstruction were also considerably aggravated. Before the war our national capital was estimated to be 52 milliard pengös or 10 milliard dollars. As a result of the war, 35 to 40% of this capital has been lost. We have lost 35% of the capital invested in our agriculture and more than half our livestock. One-third of the capital invested in industry has been lost and the other third so seriously impaired that it is useless for production. Finally, one of the most serious reasons for our postwar poverty is that two-thirds of our rolling stock was destroyed or removed by the Germans.

Those are the circumstances in which we have resumed our economic activity. We are anxious to comply with the reparation obligations we assumed under the Armistice and we have made superhuman efforts to rehabilitate our productive forces on a very modest scale. The cost of reconstruction, added to the burden of reparations—only a part of which has been paid because of the hardship prevailing in the country—has called for economic resources which, in view of the total lack of capital, can only be met by inflationary measures almost unprecedented in economic history. This inflation, mainly due to the almost total lack of commodities and the absence of the requisite State revenue, has engulfed the scanty reserves which the population had managed to retain.

Inflation in Hungary has reached such a pitch, that the Hungarian Government has been compelled to try at all costs and with no help from abroad, to stabilise the currency. This has been done, of course, at the cost of great sacrifices borne by the general population. Real wages for instance, only represent 25% of the extremely low pre-war wages level and barely a tenth of the earnings of American workmen. In the year 1946–1947, the per capita national revenue, it is estimated, will only be 350 pre-war pengös, that is 70 dollars, some 25% of which will be absorbed by taxation. The food ration, disregarding the additions for special categories of workers, will only furnish one hundred calories a day, nearly half of which will have to be obtained from UNRRA supplies.

The stabilisation budget represents the maximum effort we can achieve. The items applying to reparations, the maintenance of the Inter-allied Control Commission and the Army of Occupation account for one-third of budget expenditure and absorb 40% of the State Revenue. Even in these circumstances, the sums budgeted for reparations only suffice because the Soviet Union was good enough to allow us to make our reparations payments by instalments and to reckon against the first two annual payments the value of the Hungarian capital invested in an important concern abroad. This generosity, together with the gratitude we owe the liberators of our country, compels us to concentrate our efforts and devote all our energy to meeting our obligations.

The figures I have just quoted, will have shown you that it has been impossible to make provision in our stabilisation budget for the service of our pre-war debts and the payments involved in the restitution of Allied property as provided for in the draft treaty.

We trust that, in its wisdom, the Conference will put us in a position to meet the obligations arising out of our pre-war debts— the existence of which we formally recognise—and our other international obligations, while at the same time avoiding the further economic collapse of our country.

We will take the liberty of putting before the relevant commission, our detailed observations with the necessary supporting evidence on these problems. May I, however, venture to voice here our main idea—to find an equilibrium between the burdens and the payment capacity of a debtor country on the basis of a very modest standard of living for the population and extremely low possibilities of reconstruction of its national economy.

These objectives, modest though they are, can only be achieved with your assistance and your understanding. We therefore, ask for the support of the United Nations for the Hungarian nation, so sorely tried, in order that its efforts to rebuild its country and comply with its international undertakings may be facilitated.

Gentlemen, I do not propose to try your patience any longer and I shall therefore bring my statement to an end. The Hungarian Republic has asked me to be its mouth-piece and has also placed in me all its hopes for the future. The Hungarian people, which is trying to overcome past hindrances and present difficulties relying on its own resources, hopes for the victory of democratic principles. The immense majority of the nation desired the victory of the United Nations because they saw in it the dawn of an era of justice and the abolition of force both in international and domestic relations.

We know that the United Nations have set themselves the task not only of drawing up the treaties of Peace but, primarily and above all, the establishment of Peace. This task, however, can only be achieved if the spirit imbuing the Charter of the United Nations is also found in the treaties which are designed to bring about lasting peace. We were glad to learn that the conclusion of peace would enable us to join the United Nations Organisation. We shall apply for admission to the Organisation and we can, here and now, assure you that we will give it all the loyal co-operation of which we are capable. The presence in the new international organisation of the Soviet Union and the United States of America is a guarantee that this association of peoples will be really world-wide.

The Hungarian nation awaits your decision with confidence. It knows it will have to pass through difficult times, but it is resolved to build its future courageously. If it were disappointed, the consequences would be such as I refuse to contemplate. I would not like here to utter any words which might be interpreted as a kind of despairing appeal incompatible with the dignity of an ancient nation which has suffered much and is proud of having on occasion done good service to humanity and civilisation. I am sure that all of you will make a point of weighing carefully what you think should be laid down so as to confer again on the unhappy Hungarian people, Peace, the right of membership in a new world and the possibility of rejoining the Association of free nations.

THE PRESIDENT: The Conference has given the closest attention to the statement just delivered by the Hungarian Delegation.

The Members of this Conference will carefully examine the terms of this statement.

I beg the Secretary-General to escort the Hungarian Delegation.

(The Hungarian Delegation leaves).

M. JAN MASARYK (Czechoslovakia)—(Interpretation):

Mr. President—after listening with much attention to the somewhat surprising and unprecedented declaration just made by Hungary, an ex-enemy state, the Czecho-Slovak Delegation would like to have the opportunity of studying this declaration in detail so as to reply upon it tomorrow morning.

FIXING OF THE AGENDA

THE PRESIDENT: The Czecho-Slovak Delegate has made a proposal. Any opposition?

(Adopted).

The first item on tomorrow's agenda will therefore be the debate on the Hungarian statement.

MR. BONBRIGHT

PARIS CONFERENCE*
Paris, France

DOCUMENT NO. 25

UNITED STATES DELEGATION

August 27, 1946

MEMORANDUM OF CONVERSATION

PARTICIPANTS: Mr. Szegedy-Maszak, Hungarian Minister in Washington
Mr. F. T. Merrill

Mr. Szegedy-Maszak called this noon at his request and inquired whether the U.S. Delegation had been informed that the Yugoslavs had submitted two amendments to the Political and Territorial Commission for Hungary: (a) an exchange of populations between Yugoslavia and Hungary; and (b) regarding certain waterway rights. He appeared to be considerably agitated and expressed alarm over the "closing pincers of the reviving Little Entente against Hungary engulfed as it is in a sea of Slav people." He said that the Hungarians were fast coming to the conclusion that they were now "the most unfavored nation" and that the new proposals being made to rob Hungary of its sovereignty, particularly in matters of communications, confirmed his opinion that the time was approaching when it would have by necessity to accept its place in the Soviet sphere.

The exchange of populations proposal of the Yugoslavs had come as a complete surprise to the Hungarians, who had had no indication previously that the Yugoslavs thought it necessary to

---

*Box 97, RG-43, N.A.

raise the minorities issue. However, Szegedy-Maszak admitted that the Yugoslav proposal on the minorities was less important than their second proposal which was to the effect that Hungary should surrender certain rights in connection with the Danube and the Tisza rivers. He believed that Yugoslavia is now the spearhead of Soviet policies regarding the Danube and that this proposal is part of the larger picture.

He said that the arrival of Gero in Paris to be a member of the Hungarian Delegation was exceedingly ominous. Auer, the Hungarian Minister here, had asked the Prime Minister to replace Bolgar, the original nominee, as Deputy Chief of the Delegation in order that the Communist Party might participate in and accept responsibility for the Peace Treaty. (I don't believe that they bargained on getting the most brilliant and dangerous Communist of them all.)

Gero is the Minister of Communications, was trained in Moscow and at one time apparently occupied an important job in Soviet communications. It will be remembered that it was Gero who signed the collaboration agreement between the USSR and Hungary last August in Moscow without the authority of the Cabinet or the knowledge of Miklos, the Prime Minister. Szegedy-Maszak thought that when Bolgar had fallen ill, Rakosi had decided to sent Gero, who apparently has many connections with members of the "Soviet bloc" delegations. Szegedy-Maszak now is apprehensive that Gero will negotiate with the Yugoslavs in Paris unbeknownst to the rest of the Delegation and may sign away Hungary's water rights. He had already had several conversations with members of the Yugoslav Delegation. At this juncture Szegedy-Maszak pointed out that virtually the only bargaining point that Hungary now had outside of the "bridgehead" was its situation as "the turn-table" of Europe and that the Hungarian communications system, both rail and water, was the key to the economic federation of the Danubian states. It was this that the Soviet bloc was really after. Szegedy-Maszak said that he felt the Hungarians must hang on to this asset at any cost and certainly not to toss it away to the Yugoslavs.

FTMerrill:eb/ay

859.Konf.1946.

Translation from Hungarian

DOCUMENT NO. 26

MEMORANDUM

concerning the conversation between Envoy István Kertész and General Pope of Canada.

On September fifteenth the representative of the Canadian delegation in the Hungarian Committee, General Pope, invited me to have lunch with him in his room at the Hotel Crillon with the obvious purpose to discuss with me the controversial Hungaro-Czechoslovak questions.

After the usual courteous conversation, General Pope expressed with military frankness his opinion concerning the Hungaro-Czechoslovak dispute, especially regarding the Czechoslovak plan to expel the Hungarians. His view can be summed up as follows:

Personally he sympathized rather more with the Czechoslovaks, because Hungary belonged during both world wars to the camp of Canada's enemies, while Czechoslovakia was fighting with Canada during these most difficult times. Furthermore, ever since 1938, he, personally, as well as the Canadian people, was ashamed because of the events of Munich. All these circumstances add up to the fact that Canadians sympathize with Czechoslovakia much more than with Hungary. They understand that the Czechoslovaks finally want to have peace in their own country and with their neighbors. It is regrettable that according to the opinion of the Czechoslovaks, such peace can be achieved only through a forced transfer, but the Czechoslovaks cannot be condemned for this attitude in view of their experiences. It is a well-known fact that during the period between the two world wars the Hungarians living in Slovakia and the Hungarian government did everything to promote anti-Czechoslovak propaganda. Considering all these circumstances, only the Puritan conscience and conviction of the Canadians hinder them from voting for the Czechoslovak proposal concerning forceful transfer of the Hungarians. And the Canadians can maintain this attitude only if the Hungarian delegation makes concessions. Although the Czechoslovaks will have to make concessions too, the Hungarians will have to make considerably greater ones. In this way an agreement can be reached, and it might not be necessary to vote on the question of expulsion. Canada would much prefer this solution.

General Pope expressed the above summarized views in the course of an animated conversation. I told him that although Hungary had been dismembered in 1919 on the basis of the principle of nationality and the right to self-determination, the Hungarian population was nowhere asked whether it wanted to be detached from Hungary. Nearly one million Hungarians lived on territories which had been annexed to Czechoslovakia under various pretexts such as transportation, or strategic and economic necessity. It was quite natural that the Hungarian people was not pleased that by dismemberment of Hungary nearly one-third of all Hungarians had been separated from their mother country. The first World War produced tens of thousand of Hungarian refugees, more than 350,000. The natural dissatisfaction of these refugees as well as oppression of Hungarians in neighboring countries developed a revisionist spirit, which was used by reactionary governments for consolidation of their power.

I told General Pope that in 1919 General Smuts had agreed with Masaryk that the Csallóköz, inhabited entirely by Hungarians, should remain within Hungary, and that in return, Czechoslovakia would get a bridgehead opposite Bratislava on the right bank of the Danube. The Czechoslovak delegation at the Peace Conference disregarded this agreement and in the end Czechoslovakia obtained both the Csallóköz and the bridgehead.

The fate of the Hungarian minorities was relatively best in Czechoslovakia. The Hungarians had grievances but they did not suffer an oppression as harsh as that of the Hungarians in Yugoslavia and in Rumania. In connection with this situation, a substantial part of the Hungarians were satisfied in Czechoslovakia, which secured their living conditions in a democracy. This development explains the fact that in the period which preceded Munich, there was complete tranquility in the Hungarian regions of Czechoslovakia. I brought up several examples. It was understandable, however, that the Hungarians wished to return to Hungary, when they saw the disintegration of Czechoslovakia after Munich, when the Slovaks demanded their independence, and Poland acquired Czechoslovak territory inhabited by Poles. This was a self-evident phenomenon for which the Hungarians were not to be blamed in the past and should not to be blamed at the present. It seems especially unfair if the Great Powers would punish Hungary and the Hungarians of Slovakia in order to comfort their consciences because of Munich.

A further part of our discussion consisted of the comparison of data. Here I pointed out to General Pope that in spite of our war losses and the extermination of a large number of Jews, we cannot settle in Hungary the Hungarians from Slovakia who are mostly farmers because no land is available.

My arguments did not seem to convince completely General Pope; at best they disturbed his belief in certain Czechoslovak assertions. He told me frankly that he had been a long-time friend of several Czechoslovak delegates.

There is no doubt that my interlocutor is a man of good faith and good will who desires a Hungaro-Czechoslovak rapprochement.

DOCUMENT NO. 27
TELEGRAM SENT*

(INDEX NO. _____6_____

TO: SECSTATE
   WASHINGTON
CODE: CLEAR

DATE: September 21, 1946
NO: 4752
CHARGED TO: Allotment H-21

Yugoslav Delegation yesterday withdrew its amendment to draft treaty with Hungary which proposed exchange of populations with Hungary as an annex. Hungarian Legation Paris has issued following statement. (Odsic <u>175</u> to Dept; rpt to Budapest as <u>128</u>) QUOTE Pursuant to Yugoslav wish to come to agreement with Hungary regarding means of carrying out an exchange of minority populations, conversations have been carried out between Hungarian and Yugoslav Delegations. During these conversations the Hungarian Delegation set forth its point of view in a written document. The Yugoslav Delegation accepted the Hungarian proposal as its own, thereby emphasizing its principle objective was to work for rapprochement of the two people. According to terms of agreement, 40,000 Hungarians and similar number of Yugoslavs will be exchanged, it being understood that on both sides of the frontier full liberty of decision of interested persons will be respected. Execution of the agreement will begin one year after signature and is to be completed during three following years. Persons affected will be authorized to take their movable property and will be indemnified by their respective states for their immovable property. An official communique concerning the agreement will be made public shortly. UNQUOTE

CAFFERY

USDel:FMerrill:fg-ss

---

*Box 98, RG-43, N.A.

860. Konf. 1946.

Translation from Hungarian

DOCUMENT NO. 28

REPORT

Conversation between István Kertész, envoy extraordinary and minister plenipotentiary, and the delegate of New Zealand, Mr. Costello, on September 29, 1946.

Today as I was about to take my lunch in Hotel Claridge, the reporteur of the Hungarian Subcommittee, Mr. Costello, delegate of New Zealand, asked me to lunch with him at a separate table, indicating that he had important communications to make.

Mr. Costello started our conversation by telling me that his government had instructed him to vote in favor of the Czechoslovak proposal concerning the transfer of 200,000 Hungarians. He explained that the reason of this decision was the sympathy which the government of New Zealand felt toward Czechoslovakia. He also informed me that in the Hungarian Committee Great Britain, the United States, Australia, and the South African Union would vote against the Czechoslovak proposal. The attitude of Canada is yet undecided. The delegate of India will most probably abstain from voting. Since Nehru is Clementis' good friend, the Indian delegation will certainly not oppose the Czechoslovak proposal. The five Slav states, New Zealand, and France will vote in favor of the Czech proposal. And, if Canada and India decide to join them, a majority of two-thirds will be possible. He asked me to accept the Czechoslovak proposal through a compromise. On his part he would not find it burdensome if the transfer of 200,000 people would take place during ten years, with a yearly contingent of 20,000. But in his opinion the number might be reduced.

I told Mr. Costello, that for us the forced transfer is unacceptable under any conditions. This position is a matter of principle. We cannot make concessions even if the Czechoslovaks would designate a very low number of Hungarians to be transferred. I referred to our arguments of principle and to the practical impossibility of the execution of the transfer. Mr. Costello recognized that one cannot put farmers from Csallóköz in the place of the Jewish merchants and intellectuals of Budapest or the countryside. He did not seem to believe, however, that we have already distributed all the land of the Germans who left Hungary. He referred to the Czechoslovak assertion that we paid lip service to the agrarian reform. I explained the far-reaching provisions and radical execution of the land reform and pointed out that we still had several hundreds of thousands of people who claimed land.

After a lengthy debate over the arguments for and against the forced transfer, he asked me what we would do if the Conference voted in favor of the Czech proposal. I told Mr. Costello that in this case we probably would return home in a demonstrative way and would await further developments. When he replied that in this case we would make impossible the humane execution of the transfer, I told him that the transfer proposed by the Czechoslovaks could not be executed in a humane form. A humane transfer does not consist only of trains and heated railroad cars. We could not secure a livelihood for the tens of thousands of Hungarian peasant families. Execution of this plan would have such a catastrophic effect on the present Hungarian regime that it would collapse. It seemed to us that the Czechoslovaks did not have any interest in the stabilization of Hungarian democracy. Otherwise, they would not force such a monstrous plan.

The delegate of New Zealand expressed his fear that in case of our refusal the whole Hungarian population of Slovakia might be transferred to some remote parts of Soviet Russia. I flatly refused to entertain this possibility. We discussed several other questions concerning Hungaro-Czechoslovak relations, and some basic difficulties of the Hungarian government. Mr. Costello was depressed by our conversation, and emphasized several times, especially in parting, how "frightfully sorry" he was because of its negative result.

(signed) István Kertész

PHILIP E. MOSELY'S REVIEW OF THE VOLUMES PUBLISHED BY THE HUNGARIAN MINISTRY FOR FOREIGN AFFAIRS ON HUNGARY AND THE CONFERENCE OF PARIS* DOCUMENT NO. 29

Hungary and the Conference of Paris. Planned as a series of five volumes, in English, French, Russian and Hungarian. Volume I: *Les rapports internationaux de la Hongrie avant la Conférence de Paris,* pp. ix, 190. Volume II: *Hungary's International Relations before the Conference of Paris,* pp. xviii, 172. Volume IV: *Hungary at the Conference of Paris,* pp. xxii, 202. Budapest: Hungarian Ministry of Foreign Affairs, 1947.

As a record of its defense of Hungarian interests before and during the Paris Conference of 1946 the Hungarian Ministry of Foreign Affairs has prepared a series of five volumes, to appear in English, French, Russian, and Hungarian. Prior to the Communist seizure of power in May, 1947, three volumes had been issued, Volume I in French and Volumes II and IV in English. These volumes offer a valuable documentation of several important questions which arose in the drafting of the treaty of peace with Hungary. Their usefulness has been enhanced by careful technical presentation, including introductory surveys, indexes of persons and subjects, and maps. In view of the political overturn of May, 1947, it is unlikely that the remaining two volumes will now appear. The moving spirit in the preparation of the series, Dr. Stephen Kertész, resigned as Minister to Italy in June, 1947, and has recently held temporary positions at Yale and Notre Dame universities.

Volume I presents a brief survey of the preparation for the peace-making, begun clandestinely under Nazi occupation and continued at Debrecen and Budapest after the armistice. A series of eight long notes, between July 4, 1945, and May 8, 1946, reviews the larger questions of the future settlement, placing major emphasis upon the need for promoting Danubian coöperation in economic development, land and river transportation, cultural life, and the protection of minorities. This emphasis could hardly have pleased the Soviet foreign office, with its phobia of regional group-

---

Journal of Central European Affairs, Vol. 8 (October 1948), 317–19.

ings beyond its direct control. In the light of the well-disciplined functioning of the Soviet bloc at the Belgrade Conference of 1948 it is ironical to find the Hungarian government, in a note of November 12, 1945, urging the revival and strengthening of international control over the Danube, with continued participation of non-riparian states in an effectively functioning commission.

Three memoranda deal with Hungarian-Rumanian relations. Under date of April 27, 1946, the Hungarian government proposed a territorial change in the Transylvanian frontier, which would have returned 22,000 sq. km. to Hungary, leaving 865,000 Rumanians in Hungary and 1,060,000 Magyars in Rumania. Other memoranda deal with the grievances of the Hungarian minority and the question of rights of citizenship. In a memorandum of June 11, 1946, addressed to the Council of Foreign Ministers, the Hungarian government urged the importance of reviving and strengthening provisions for the international protection of minority rights, with the system of mixed commissions and tribunals to enforce them. On August 30, the Hungarian delegation in Paris circulated an elaborate draft treaty for the protection of minority rights.

The Hungarian government asked without success to be admitted to discuss the future treaty prior to the Paris Conference. On January 25, 1946, it suggested the creation of an allied commission of experts to consult with it on these problems. On June 12, it asked again for a hearing by the Council of Foreign Ministers. Actually, by that time several of the basic questions, such as reparations, abandonment of the pre-war guarantees of minority rights, and restoration of the pre-war Hungarian-Rumanian frontier, had been decided in the Council of Foreign Ministers, without the Hungarian case having received a hearing.

Volume II deals with Hungarian-Czechoslovak relations prior to the Paris Conference, in particular with the future of the Magyar minority in Slovakia. A request of September 12, 1945, for a hearing on this question was ignored by the Council of Foreign Ministers. The documents describe in some detail the Hungarian-Czechoslovak negotiations of December, 1945, and February, 1946, leading up to the agreement of February 27 for the exchange of Slovaks repatriated voluntarily from Hungary against an equal number of Magyars to be transferred from Slovakia. In a letter of February 27 the Czechoslovak government again affirmed its determination to expel another 200,000 to 250,000 Hungarians, without pretense of exchange, and to "re-Slovakize" the remaining members of the minority. Other documents present lengthy exchanges of accusations in connection with the execution of the agreement, together with an Hungarian appeal to the Great Powers.

Volume IV carries the same problem through the Paris Conference. By reproducing speeches, memoranda, and excerpts from minutes, it traces the struggle which developed over the Czechoslovak effort, supported by the Soviet bloc, to insert into the recommendations of the Conference a provision for the outright transfer of 200,000 Hungarians. At the climax of the controversy the Hungarian delegation offered, on September 30, to accept two-thirds of the minority with the territory on which they lived and one-third without territorial compensation. The upshot was a rather meaningless recommendation, opposed at Paris by the Soviet bloc but later accepted in the Hungarian treaty, which referred the question to direct negotiation between the Czechoslovak and Hungarian governments. Annex I to this volume reproduces a carefully documented Hungarian memorandum of 47 pages on the question of the Hungarians in Slovakia.

Volume III, which has apparently not been published, was to contain materials relating to all political questions treated at the Paris Conference except those relating to the Hungarians in Slovakia. Volume V, likewise not available, was to cover economic questions involved in the drafting of the treaty.

The general impression left by the three volumes so far published is that the Hungarian government had prepared its case with care on the assumption that the issues would be treated on their merits by the Great Powers, all of them concerned primarily with promoting peace and stability in the Danubian region. In the procedural and substantive tussles of the Paris Conference this assumption proved ill-founded. The struggle over the formal terms of the treaty was merely one aspect of a more general struggle to extend or confine Soviet power in Europe. In that struggle Hungary had little to hope for and much to fear.

PHILIP E. MOSELY

The Russian Institute of Columbia University

The Expulsion of the Germans from Hungary: A Study in Postwar Diplomacy*

DOCUMENT NO. 30

I

The key to the problem of the expulsion of the Germans from Hungary was the Potsdam Conference, where the representatives of the three major Allies declared "that the transfer to Germany of German populations, or elements thereof remaining in Poland, Czechoslovakia and Hungary, will have to be undertaken." Thus the three major Allies assimilated the problem of the Germans in Hungary with the problems of Germans in Poland and Czechoslovakia, although in reality the situation in Hungary differed greatly from that in the other two countries. The terms of the Potsdam decision might have been suitable for the Polish and Czechoslovak situations, but were most misleading when applied to Hungary.

Poland and Czechoslovakia, as members of the winning team, emphatically demanded the removal of their entire German population, and actually expelled a substantial portion of these people long before the Potsdam Conference convened. This harsh procedure was the reaction against Nazi policies and cruelties. Under Nazi leadership some Germans committed in occupied countries crimes of a most brutal nature, and the shadow of these crimes had fallen upon the whole German people. In Germany the scoundrels and psycopaths dominated the country because they were more determined and audacious than the decent and balanced individuals. The majority of the German people undoubtedly tolerated Nazi abuses.

But in a totalitarian dictatorship under modern world conditions popular uprisings are extremely difficult if not impossible.

*The Review of Politics, Vol. 15, (1953), 179-208.

Moreover, not all Nazis were common criminals and not all Germans were Nazis. Some of them opposed Hitlerism at the risk of their own lives. The indiscriminate application of collective responsibility upon all Germans seems not only unjustified but also an efficient boomerang of Western moral principles and political expectations. Collective punishment administered against entire ethnic groups undoubtedly violates the basic tenets of Christianity. When, however, human passion rides the crest of waves, moral principles and political wisdom are often thrown overboard. *Actio parit reactionem,* sometimes on a very great magnitude.

Politically, the case for all-out German deportation could be argued in support of Poland's action since her frontiers had been extended *de facto* with the consent of the three major victorious powers to the Oder-Neisse line as a compensation for the territories lost in the East to the Soviet Union. The wartime attitude of the Germans in Poland created the necessary political climate for such action. The exodus of the Poles from territories attached to the Soviet Union was an additional reason given for this policy.

Much less justification can be found for the *indiscriminate* deportation of the Germans in the case of Czechoslovakia and Hungary, where the peace settlement made no changes in German-inhabited frontiers. Nevertheless, the Czechoslovak Government decided to get rid of all their non-Slavic nationalities and began the drastic execution of this policy at the close of hostilities.

A strong anti-Nazi feeling existed in Hungary as well, but the new Hungarian regime did not adopt the same policy as Poland and Czechoslovakia. No German was expelled from the country before Potsdam, and the Hungarian Government, prompted by Soviet summons, asked for the removal of only those Germans who were disloyal to Hungary.

The Soviet drive for the total expulsion of the Germans from Hungary and the arguments of the Hungarian Communist Party gained momentum through the Potsdam agreement and through its implementation by the Allied Control Council for Germany. Although Hungary took a stand against the principle of collective responsibility, in view of the sweeping and ambiguous terms of these inter-Allied decisions, it was difficult for a defeated state to maintain this position.

During the Second World War, the Hungarian Government deprived of their citizenship all Hungarian nationals who enlisted in the *SS* forces. This unique policy in Danubian Europe was maintained until the German occupation of Hungary on March 19, 1944. At the same time, the political division of the Foreign Ministry collected data describing the fifth-column activities of certain German minority groups in southeastern Europe in general and in Hungary in particular. Experts were assigned to prepare confidential memoranda on the same subject. This material was intended to be used at a peace conference under the leadership of the Western powers. Such expectations, however, did not materialize and in the postwar era the political significance of the German minority in Hungary changed. In view of the Russian and Communist attitude, the anti-German material of the Foreign Ministry was scrapped and never used.

This policy was particularly strengthened by the fact that the expulsion of the Germans from Hungary was linked to the expulsion of the Hungarians from Czechoslovakia. Even before the Potsdam decision, various Czechoslovakian spokesmen argued that the expulsion of the Germans from Hungary would make possible the resettlement in Hungary of the Hungarians living in Slovakia, whose removal was resolved by the Czechoslovak Government and strongly supported by the Soviet Union.

II

In the course of the occupation of Hungary the attitude of the Red Army toward the German population of Hungary[1] underwent some changes. In Eastern Hungary almost the entire adult population of some villages inhabited by people of German origin was deported to Russia. This action was directed against the Germans or against people of German origin. When, however, the Red Army reached the great German settlements in Hungary, this attitude changed. Specific action directed against the Germans ceased and civilians in great numbers were deported to Russia irrespective of their ethnic origins. While in Rumania and in Yugoslavia, the Red Army deported the Germans on a much larger scale for forced labor in the Soviet Union,[2] the Russian policy in Hungary took a different turn. It did not stop with the deportations carried out by the Red Army but was followed by political actions of the Soviet representatives in Hungary, and by the Soviet delegation at Potsdam.

In early 1945, Marshal Klementy Voroshilov, the Chairman of the Allied Control Commission in Hungary (hereafter ACC), urged the Hungarian Government to prepare measures for the wholesale expulsion of the Germans. The Soviet political representative, Georgij Pushkin, repeatedly brought up the matter with the Hungarian Foreign Minister, János Gyöngyösi. Pushkin demanded that Hungary request the expulsion of the Germans. The Russian argument was that the removal of the Germans would be a great benefit to Hungary because it would relieve the country from a dangerous fifth column and would eliminate once and for all the possibility of German interference in Hungarian domestic affairs through the pretext of protecting a German minority.

Following these Russian demands, the Council of Ministers and an interparty meeting discussed the problem in May, 1945. Although the Communist Party and the National Peasant Party supported the wholesale deportation of the Germans, the Hungarian authorities took a stand against indiscriminate deportations on the basis of collective responsibility. It was agreed that only the disloyal Germans should be deprived of their citizenship and, after the confiscation of their property, expelled from Hungary.[3]

Although these decisions were taken under Soviet pressure, there existed in Hungary after the Second World War a genuine and fairly general anti-German feeling. Hungary had suffered under Nazi occupation since March 19, 1944. A considerable part of the German population in the country was Hitlerite and had played the treacherous role of a fifth column. But, at the same time, a great many Germans opposed the Hitlerite ideology. They even organized a "loyalty movement." Non-Communist political leaders tried to defend the interests of this latter group and to limit expulsion to those Germans who took an active part in Nazi movements. Even for this group, transfer to Germany seemed a better fate than their possible deportation to the Soviet Union.

Following these Soviet initiatives, Foreign Minister Gyöngyösi addressed a letter to Pushkin on May 16, 1945, which stated that according to the opinion of Ferenc Erdei, Minister of Interior,[4] the members of the Volksbund to be expelled numbered around 300,000. The official note of the Hungarian Government addressed to the Government of the Soviet Union on May 26, 1945, set forth that "it would be necessary to transfer from Hungary those Germans who became the servants of Hitlerism and traitors to Hungary's cause because this would be the only way to assure that the German spirit and oppression could not dominate the country any longer." The same note stated that the number of such Nazi-Germans might be 200,000–250,000.

I had no knowledge of either the letter or the note until early August, 1945, when the Foreign Minister informed me that Marshal Voroshilov demanded from the Hungarian Government urgent preparations to implement plans for the transfer of 400,000 Germans from Hungary. We did not know at that time the terms of the Potsdam Agreement, and I was astonished to hear this high figure. Immediately I prepared a memorandum which proved that the number of the Germans to be transferred on the basis of participation in Nazi movements would not be higher than the number given in the note of May 26, that is, 200,000–250,000. I pointed out that acceptance of the Hitlerite principle of collective responsibility would create a most dangerous precedent which could be used against Hungarian minorities in neighboring countries. In further arguments I relied greatly on an American memorandum of June 12, 1945, and on our reply to it. Both took a stand against application of the principle of collective responsibility to ethnic groups.[5]

The Foreign Minister asked me to go to see the Minister of Interior, Erdei, who was charged with preparing the expulsion of the 400,000 Germans, and to convince him of the impracticability of the project. I explained to Erdei the content of my memorandum and proved to him that the number of the Germans to be expelled on the basis of their participation in Nazi movements could by no means exceed the number 200,000–250,000. I added that the transfer of the Germans from Hungary was obviously connected with the transfer of the Hungarians from Czechoslovakia. The Czechoslovaks from the very beginning of their anti-Hungarian campaign had used the argument that with the expulsion of the Germans there would be ample space in Hungary for the Hungarians to be transferred from Czechoslovakia. Consequently, I argued, this was an additional reason why we should reduce as much as possible the number of the Germans to be expelled from Hungary.

Erdei did not question the correctness of my data and arguments. He simply replied that the expulsion of the Germans was a Russian order which we could not resist. As to the transfer of the Hungarians from Czechoslovakia, this plan was backed also by Russia. So we simply had to accept the removal of about half a million Hungarians.

With such a large scale deportation of Germans, he argued, we would at least make possible the resettlement of the unfortunate Hungarians to be transferred from Slovakia.

The position of the Foreign Ministry was supported by leading Smallholder politicians. This resistance delayed somewhat the prepa- rations of the Ministry of Interior but could not change the course of events.

III

Hungarian opposition to a large scale German expulsion was fatally weakened by the Potsdam Agreement. At the Potsdam Conference, in a surprise move, the Soviet delegation proposed that provision for the expulsion of the Germans from Hungary should be inserted into Article XIII which dealt with the expulsion of the Germans from Poland and Czechoslovakia.[6] Thus, the Soviet policymakers had obtained final Western endorsement of the expulsion of the Germans from Czechoslovakia, Poland and Hungary. Although the report on the Tripartite Conference was announced on August 2, the Hungarian Foreign Ministry received an authentic text of it only much later and—characteristically enough—in Russian. In 1945, we were almost completely isolated from the West, did not receive foreign newspapers regularly, and had no representatives abroad. We were supposed to get official communication from the Allied powers through the ACC, but actually were left in the dark concerning many international events directly affecting Hungary's fate.

From this time onward, Article XIII of the Potsdam Agreement became the basis for the expulsion of the Germans. Whether this text was intended to be an authorization, suggestion, or a polite order with the endorsement of the principle of collective responsi- bility, was a matter of interpretation. In any case, the political and legal position of Hungary was quite different from that of Poland and Czechoslovakia. The latter states belonged to the victorious powers and they emphatically demanded the removal of their entire German population. Hungary, as a former Axis satellite, lived under the supervision of the ACC. The Hungarian Govern- ment asked, under Russian pressure, for the removal of only those Germans "who became traitors to Hungary's cause." But Hungary never asked for a total transfer on the basis of collective responsibility.

The Potsdam text was all the more bewildering for Hungary because the above-mentioned American memorandum of June 12, 1945, took a resolute stand against the principle of collective responsibility. Until Potsdam we thought that Western policy was based on this stand. Article XIII of the Potsdam Agreement, however, seemed to contradict this assumption.

Later the motives of the American attitude at Potsdam were clarified, to some extent. In 1950, a report of a special subcommittee of the Committee on the Judiciary of the House of Representatives dealt with the problem of expellees and refugees of German ethnic origin.[7] This report pointed out that the United States delegation at Potsdam supported the provisions regarding German expellees not because it wanted to sponsor the mass expulsion.

> *The United States delegation, led by the President of the United States, agreed to the wording of article XIII solely because it wanted* (1) *to make more orderly and humane the inevitable expulsion of those Germans who still remained in eastern Europe, and* (2) *to open occupied Germany to those who were faced with deportation to remote sub-Arctic territories of Soviet Russia, an equivalent to annihilation. The records of the Potsdam Conference make these facts plain.*[8]

This report or any other official text, however, failed to give any reason whatever for the inclusion in the Potsdam text of the Germans in Hungary. Moreover, if the American delegation refused to accept the principle of collective responsibility, such a reserve could have been inserted into the Potsdam Agreement.

The good faith and good intentions of the American delegation at Potsdam are unquestionable. According to the principles of Roman law, however, *De internis non judicat praetor,* and to the ways of diplomacy, intentions not appearing clearly in a written text can be interpreted in many different ways. Semantics are an especially baffling problem in relationships with Communist-dominated countries. The phrase that the transfer of German populations "will have to be undertaken," was not mitigated by any qualifying statement in the Potsdam Agreement or in a separate British or American declaration. The decision concerning the "orderly and humane" effectuation of the transfers is certainly commendable, but this was only a procedural matter. Western opposition to the application of collective punishment was not publicly expressed at the time. Certain principles are true without saying, but sometimes this is not a reason for not stating them.

The attitude of the Allied Control Council for Germany toward the problems of the Germans in Hungary was even more amazing. In accordance with the Potsdam Agreement, the Allied Control Council, on November 20, 1945, approved a plan for the transfer of the German population of Austria, Czechoslovakia, Hungary and Poland to the four occupied zones of Germany. This plan outlined the tentative allocation between zones of occupation and a schedule of movement of the German population in the following manner:

Of the 3,500,000 Germans to be expelled from Poland, 2,000,000 were to be admitted into the Soviet Zone of occupation and 1,500,000 into the British Zone. Of the 2,500,000 Germans to be moved from Czechoslovakia, 1,750,000 were to be admitted into the American Zone and 750,000 into the Soviet Zone; 500,000 Germans from Hungary were to be admitted into the American Zone and 150,000 Germans were to be moved from Austria into the French Zone in Germany. Execution of the plan was to begin in November, 1945, and was to be completed by August 1, 1946.[9]

The insertion into this inter-Allied decision of the figure of 500,000 Germans "to be moved" from Hungary was a new development. The total number of Germans in Hungary was considerably less and a substantial portion had moved to Germany with the retreating Germany Army in 1944. Even if this figure was proposed by the Soviet representative, it would have been possible to ascertain the accurate data through the American and British missions in Budapest.

Thus, an inter-Allied agreement doubled the number of the 250,000 potential German expellees, a number indicated by the note of the Hungarian Foreign Ministry on May 26, 1945. The Russians were probably dissatisfied with this Hungarian offer and intended to obtain a more sweeping result by inter-Allied agreements. In this they succeeded.

After Potsdam, the Soviet authorities in Hungary negotiated directly with the Prime Minister and the Minister of Interior. Voroshilov as Chairman of the ACC was not obligated to deal with Hungarian authorities through the Foreign Ministry and in practice often avoided all contact with it.

According to the diary of General William S. Key, American representative in the ACC,[10] Marshal Voroshilov informed the Commission at its meeting on November 26, 1945, that he had received from his Government a plan for the deportation of the Swabians[11] to Germany, a plan approved by the Allied Control Council for Germany. The Swabians were to be transferred from Hungary to the United States Zone of Germany. The movement was to begin in December and to be continued over a period of eight months. This was the first reference, made in the ACC, to the removal of the Swabians from Hungary. Subsequently the American and British representatives received certain instructions from their governments, but the Hungarian Foreign Ministry was left in the dark.

IV

It was toward the end of November, 1945, that I read in the newspapers the statement of Foreign Secretary Bevin (made in the House of Commons on November 23), about the German expulsions and the decision of the Allied Control Council in Germany. Some newspapers announced that Hungary was obligated to expel 500,000 Germans.

It seemed to me that such an inter-Allied decision was a most serious blow to our efforts aiming at the reduction of the number of Germans to be expelled. All figures given so far by the Hungarian authorities were much lower and it was difficult to understand Western approval for the doubling of the Hungarian figures, and for adding 100,000 to the 400,000 demanded by Voroshilov. In the light of such a Western attitude, our resistance to Soviet demands did not seem very promising. I wanted to make clear the Hungarian position and immediately drafted a note of protest which was dispatched to the British, United States and Soviet political missions on December 1, 1945. This note outlined the core of the problem as follows:

> Certain news items published in the Press indicate that those competent to settle the problems of Central-Europe are misinformed about the number of Germans in Hungary and, what is more, about the number of

Germans who may be expatriated from Hungary under the principles adopted by the victorious Great Powers. For this reason the Hungarian Government consider it as their obligation to inform the Government of the United States of America about the following:

Census figures of 1941 indicate that the number of people of German vernacular on the territory of Hungary amounted to 477,057, while those of German nationality to 303,419.

The difference between the two figures is considerable and due to the fact that amongst those of German vernacular were numerous elements of Jewish or non-German descents, moreover many of German descent and German vernacular entered their name on the census sheets as being of Hungarian nationality. This latter attitude meant their definitive rupture with Germanism and open confession on the side of Hungary in 1941, the heyday of German victories, just in the period of increasing German pressure and terror. Indeed, there is a considerable number of people of German descent and German vernacular who were willing to share the fate of Hungarians even in the period of the severest German oppression, many of them having participated also in the resistance movement of the democratic parties.

Another part of the note evaluated the results of the special procedure undertaken to investigate the national loyalty of Germans in Hungary and suggested that the number of the Germans to be expatriated hardly exceeded 200,000. Then the note concluded:

Considering the fact that the most compromised Germans, and especially a considerable part of the German male population, left the territory of the country together with the beaten German army, it seems to be probable that 200,000 to 250,000 will prove to be a realistic figure of the German population to be expatriated, as it has been intimated in the note of the 26th May, 1945, addressed by the Hungarian Government to the Government of the Soviet Union.

The Government of democratic Hungary avail themselves of this opportunity to state that it would be contrary to their convictions that Hungarian citizens should be expatriated solely on account of their ethnic origin. They are averse as well to this as to any kind of collective punishment. For this reason they consider it desirable that only those Germans should be expatriated who were manifest traitors to the cause of Hungary by their attitude of having served Hitlerism . . . [12]

After dispatching this note, I accompanied Foreign Minister Gyöngyösi to Prague in order to negotiate the proposed Hungaro-Slovak population exchange, pressed on Hungary by the Czechoslovak Government and the Soviet Union. Vladimir Clementis, undersecretary of state in the Czechoslovak Foreign Ministry, pointed out in his address of welcome that after the execution of the Hungaro-Slovak population exchange, Czechoslovakia intended to expel the remaining Hungarians who were not subject to the exchange.[13] Although the Hungarian Delegation refused to negotiate on the removal of the Hungarians from Czechoslovakia, the connection between the expulsion of the Germans from Hungary and the expulsion of the Hungarians from Czechoslovakia was made once more absolutely clear. President Beneš went even further in declaring to Foreign Minister Gyöngyösi that the three major Allies agreed in principle at Potsdam on the removal of the Germans and Hungarians from Czechoslovakia, and he was rather astonished to see that the Hungarians were stubbornly resisting the implementation of this policy.[14]

Although the official Potsdam text did not support Beneš' contention, tacit and unpublished understandings are not unknown in diplomacy. Thus I thought it necessary to obtain some clarification. Upon my return to Budapest, I went to see the American Minister to Hungary, H. F. Arthur Schoenfeld, and informed him about President Beneš' statement. I also mentioned that in view of the Potsdam text and the November 20 decision of the Allied Control Council, it might be the responsibility of the Western powers—should Hungary expel the Germans on the basis of collective responsibility. Schoenfeld stated that at Potsdam no agreement whatever was made concerning the expulsion of the Hungarians from Czechoslovakia, and he categorically denied the validity of the interpretation that the inter-Allied decisions amounted to an endorsement of the principle of collective responsibility.

His answer was reassuring, but the first American note (dated December 4, 1945), which we received in connection with the transfer of the Germans, contained only general information. It summed up the unhappy experience with German refugees entering Germany from areas east of the Oder-Neisse Line,[15] and informed us that:

> ... the Control Council in Berlin has adopted a program for the orderly and humane transfer of the German populations from Poland, Czechoslovakia and Hungary. The satisfactory fulfillment of this plan will be jeopardized by the uncontrolled movements of these peoples and the threat of epidemics may force suspension of its operation indefinitely.

The note concluded that the United States Mission was "gratified to observe" that the Hungarian Government in its note of November 9 had "accepted the principles agreed to at Potsdam," and that "the transfer of certain numbers of the German minority from Hungary" could be carried out "in an orderly humane manner."

Thus the American note blandly emphasized lofty principles, but did not deal at all with our fundamental problems, which were connected with the number of Germans to be expelled and the standards to be applied in the course of their selection. The Potsdam Agreement and the decision of the Allied Control Council of November 20, had confused the situation and played directly into the hands of Czechoslovakia and the Soviet Union.

In order to secure an immediate written statement from the English-speaking powers, I reiterated in a *Note Verbale* of December 15, 1945, our opposition to collective punishment of the Germans and pointed out that the Hungarian Government never planned "a transfer based on the mere fact of German origin, or speaking German as the mother tongue, which would mean a removal equalling collective punishment." The note referred again to the rumors that "the Allied Powers are planning to oblige Hungary to remove 500,000 Germans" and requested an official statement concerning the ultimate position of the British and United States Governments.[16] This *Note Verbale* was not sent to the Soviet Mission since the position of the Soviet Union was only too clear in the matter.

Meanwhile, the Hungarian Ministry of Interior made preparations for the total expulsion of the Germans, according to the Russian wishes. On December 20, Foreign Minister Gyöngyösi informed me that the Council of Ministers soon would deal with problems concerning expulsion of the Germans and gave me the draft of the decree which he just had received. The first article of the text declared:

> Those Hungarian citizens who declared themselves of German vernacular or of German nationality at the last census, those who changed back their magyarized names into the original German, those who were members of the *Volksbund* or of a German armed formation [*SS*] are subject to obligatory transfer into Germany.

It is true that another paragraph made possible the exemption from transfer of those persons who in the years past, actively supported a democratic party; but the maximum number of such exemptions was limited to ten percent of all Germans falling under the compulsory transfer in a community. Moreover, the Minister of Interior, Erdei, was authorized to appoint a committee to decide definitively in all cases of exemption. In view of Erdei's allegiance to the Communist Party, this provision in practice meant exemption for those opportunists who entered the Communist Party or served the Communist cause otherwise.

When I received the draft, I first expressed my objections to the Foreign Minister orally, and the next day prepared a memorandum the main points of which were as follows:

1. The Hungarian Government in its decrees and notes addressed to foreign powers has always indicated so far that it refused and will refuse to implement any kind of collective punishment, and that it will inflict penalties only upon those Germans, who, by their individual conduct, have betrayed Hungary. . . .
2. Irrespective of this internally and externally taken stand, the construction and the spirit of the decree bear a close resemblance to the anti-Jewish measures of the Nazi-regime. Probably its execution would not be different either.
3. It is of greatest danger from the national point of view that this decree might be used by the neighboring states as a precedent and an example for possible actions against

Hungarian minorities. . . . We would have no moral basis for our own defense if we were to create such a precedent for forcible transfer based on the mother tongue and nationality.

4. If the transfer of the Germans would start on such a wide basis, and later on would be discontinued for some reason, it would be quite possible that masses of former members of the *Volksbund* would remain in the country and a great number of persons of German vernacular who declared themselves Hungarian in 1941 and even people of Hungarian mother tongue could be expelled.

5. Again, mother tongue cannot form a basis for expulsion, because among persons of German vernacular there are a number of other nationalities, for example, Jews.

6. Irrespective of many legal weaknesses of the draft—which I pointed out by way of numerous examples—it is almost certain that, because of the lack of means of transportation, of food and of fuel, it would not be possible to execute the transfer in an orderly and humane manner, as prescribed by the Potsdam decision. The responsibility for the shortcomings of such a procedure would fall back exclusively on the Hungarian Government and the Hungarian people. Thus, we would have no moral right any more to protest against the expulsion of the Hungarians from Czechoslovakia.

The rest of the memorandum proposed a new text which would have based the transfer on individual responsibility—as expressed in our previous notes addressed to the major Allied powers.

The Foreign Minister shared my views expressed in the memorandum and read its text in the Council of Ministers on December 22. However, after a long debate, he was voted down. Only five Smallholder ministers voted with him.[17] The Communist leader, Mátyás Rákosi, and Prime Minister Zoltán Tildy, who carried the majority, argued that no matter what our own point of view had been in the past, Hungary by this decree, was only executing the order of the victorious great powers as expressed in the Potsdam Agreement, and in the decision of the Allied Control Council for Germany on November 20. In harmony with this view, the decree began with the introduction:

The Ministerium, in executing the decision of the Allied Control Council of November 20 . . . ordains the following: . . .

A few days later I addressed a memorandum to Prime Minister Tildy concerning the Hungarian peace preparations, and in this text I protested against the decree in the following terms:

> For a defeated small country, it is of fundamental importance, almost to the question of survival, to profess consistently certain fundamental moral, legal and political principles. Only in this way is it possible to win the support, understanding and respect of the civilized world.
>
> Therefore, the decision of the Hungarian Government concerning the expulsion of individuals of German mother tongue or nationality, might have disastrous impact on the development of our international position. We repeatedly made solemn statements to foreign powers to the effect that all expulsions would be made on the basis of individual and not on collective responsibility. Irrespective of these pledges, the government decided to promulgate a decree which entirely contradicted our former policy statements.
>
> This decision is all the more regrettable because the acceptance of the principle of collective responsibility might have a boomerang effect on the Hungarians living in the neighboring states. As a result, we shall miss in the future the principle which assured for us an unassailable moral superiority at the negotiations at Prague.
>
> It is worthwhile to mention in this connection that the foreign policy of the great powers usually does not change basically, from one day to the other, in the fields of fundamental moral and political principles. A small and defeated country can afford such changes even less because its only strength lies in the consistent adherence to moral principles appealing to the whole civilized world.
>
> If the Hungarian government would continue to demonstrate such an unstable and inconsequent attitude in fundamental questions, then we would have no serious basis on which to build and the whole preparatory peace work might prove to be a useless endeavor. In any case, the government with this decision opened the way to the arguments which could be brought against us and with this step took the burden of an historical responsibility, yet of incalculable magnitude. *Videant Consules . . .* [18]

In early January, we received an American note which replied to our *Note Verbale* of December 15, 1945. The *Note* expressed the opinion that the decision of November 20, by the Allied Control Council was nothing but a general line of conduct and did not oblige the Hungarian Government to expel all the Germans or precisely 500,000 Germans. On the contrary, a reduction of this number by the Hungarian Government would be welcomed by the United States. The view of the United States concerning the non-applicability of the principle of collective responsibility to an entire ethnic group—such as the Germans in Hungary—had not changed merely because certain members of this group took part in Nazi activities. For this reason, the *Note* concluded, the United States Government was of the opinion that an ethnic group, like the Germans in Hungary, could not be punished by expulsion.

This latest condemnation of the principle of collective responsibility was in harmony with the content of the aforementioned American memorandum of June 12, 1945, but was hardly in accordance with the Potsdam Agreement. History will evaluate the reason for the lack of clarity, if not inconsistency, of American policy which in June, 1945, condemned the principle of collective responsibility in Budapest, but later in July, 1945, at the Potsdam Conference failed to uphold the same principle. The decision of the Allied Control Council of November 20, 1945, in respect to the number of Germans to be expelled from Hungary, indicates that the three major Allies did not object to the application of collective punishment against German minority groups. After the decree concerning the expulsion of the Germans was issued in Hungary, the renewal of the American stand against collective responsibility was not of much practical consequence.

A few weeks later at an inter-party conference called to discuss our peace aims, the issue which occasioned the longest debate involved the decree of December 22, 1945, concerning the deportation of the Germans from Hungary. I represented the peace preparatory division of the Foreign Ministry at this conference and pointed out again that this decree was a fundamental mistake from the point of view of our peace preparations and national interests, and asked for its revision. Moreover, I stated that the Potsdam Agreement and the decision of the Allied Control Council did not imply the endorsement of collective responsibility of all Germans and referred in this respect to the officially expressed American view. Rákosi replied to my explanations that the Americans at Potsdam clearly endorsed the principle of collective responsibility with respect to the expulsion of the Germans from Poland, Czechoslovakia and Hungary, and that this fact could not be changed by their ulterior white-washing maneuvers. He pointed out that the number of Germans to be expelled was not put without reason at 500,000 by the Allied Control Council and that Hungary as a defeated state was in no position to put forward arguments against the wishes of the victorious great powers or to speculate much about them. This was an order, even though it was couched in polite diplomatic language. Answering a question of mine, Rákosi emphasized that even Jews and other nationalities of German vernacular must be expelled. Otherwise the door would be left open for countless exceptions. In regard to my further objections to acceptance of the principle of collective responsibility, he simply replied that the cabinet, at its meeting on December 22, should have voted him down if his interpretation of the Potsdam text was wrong. Prime Minister Tildy again supported Rákosi's arguments.

During those days, the Hungarian authorities declined all objections to and responsibility for the expulsion by stating that Hungary as a defeated state merely executed the orders of the Allied Control Council—as this was expressed in the decree itself. This attitude of putting the responsibility squarely on the Allied Powers provoked American reaction. Since the Russians had achieved their objectives with the promulgation of the decree on the German expulsion, nothing hindered Marshal Voroshilov from making thereafter common cause with the Americans. He endorsed an American proposal aiming at eliminating that part of the decree which designated the Hungarian measure as an execution of the order of the Allied Powers. The American move took place at the meeting of the ACC on January 25, 1946. The diary of General William B. Key, American representative in the ACC, gives the following description of this event:

> I pointed out that the Hungarian Government's decree for the removal of the Swabians stated that it was by a decision of the ACC, which left the impression that we were responsible for the deportation. I proposed that the Hungarian Government be directed to change this decree

to show that they themselves initiated this movement and sought the cooperation from our Governments to accomplish it, which was approved at Potsdam. The Marshal agreed and stated that he would direct the Hungarian Government to re-write the decree to state the truth and also make appropriate correction in the press and also stated that the responsibility for selecting the Swabians was solely that of the Hungarian Government, that all the ACC did was to see that humane measures were observed in the movement and that they were received by the U.S. authorities in their area in Germany.

Actually, in a note to the Hungarian Government, Marshal Voroshilov demanded that the reference to the decision of the Allied Control Council should be omitted from the decree of December 22, 1945. However, as far as I have been able to ascertain, the Hungarian Government never made this change. Gyöngyösi gave some oral explanations to Pushkin. Both of them knew the real background of the affair. Much later, in a declaration issued on August 31, 1946, concerning the resumption of the suspended Swabian expatriation, the Ministry of Interior stated that the Potsdam Agreement had given to the Hungarian Government "the right to expatriate the German population of Hungary into Germany. The expatriation is not mandatory for the Hungarian Government, but the Potsdam Agreement accords the right to do it." If the ACC or at least one of the Western powers would have made such a clear public statement in autumn 1945, it is very unlikely that the Hungarian Government could have been induced to issue a decree based on collective responsibility of the German minority. Western insistence on clarity in the matter was decidedly late.

The real Russian interpretation of the figure of 500,000 Germans and the close connection between the expulsion of the Hungarians from Czechoslovakia and the expulsion of the Germans from Hungary was revealed once more at the peace negotiations. Soviet Russia openly sponsored a Czechoslovak proposal to insert in the peace treaty a provision authorizing expulsion of 200,000 Hungarians from Czechoslovakia. A. Y. Vyshinsky in a speech delivered at a session of the Political and Territorial Commission for Hungary on September 20, 1946, supported the Czechoslovak proposal with the following argument:

500,000 Germans from Hungary must be transferred to the American zone in Germany—and I am very happy that Mr. Smith, who through his military work in Germany knows this subject perfectly well, is present. This is the plan approved by the Control Council for Germany: 500,000 Germans must be transferred from Hungary to Germany into the American zone. The second question is: if these 500,000 people are transferred from Hungary to Germany, will there be room enough left in Hungary for 200,000 Hungarians, transferred from Czechoslovakia? I think there will be. We must bear in mind that on the 1st of September, 1946, only 136,847 people altogether were transferred from Hungary, that is 27.4% of the amount given in the above-mentioned plan. Consequently, if the plan for the transfer of the Germans from Hungary is carried out, it will be possible to settle in their place Hungarians from Czechoslovakia. There should be no objection therefore on the part of the Hungarian Government to receive Hungarians in place of Germans. Does it not seem strange that under these conditions, the proposal of the Czechoslovak Government met with such opposition from the Hungarian Government?[19]

V

The transfer of the Germans began in January, 1946, and the manner in which it was carried out fully justified our grave apprehensions.[20] General Lucius D. Clay summed up his impressions of the first period of the transfer in the following way:

The movement started in January, 1946. The first trainload from Hungary was a pitiful sight. The expellees had been assembled without a full allowance of food and personal baggage, and arrived hungry and destitute. As a result of representations repeated many times, arrangements were made to permit a small baggage allowance and to provide each expellee with RM 500.[21]

Undoubtedly some of the difficulties which arose in the course of removal of the Germans were the consequences of the conditions existing in Hungary. The country had been looted by the Germans and by the Russians and had had to feed the occupying Red Army. These circumstances did not facilitate carrying out the orderly transfer of the Germans. In spite of many shortcomings, including the abuses of Communist organizers and executors, the transfers from Hungary took place under better conditions than similar actions in other countries.[22] A further consideration is that forceful deportations never can be humane in the proper sense of the word even if physical comfort were assured during the journey, and the deported people were allowed to take some belongings with them.

In the course of the transfer of the Germans, the Communist Party continued to advocate an all-out deportation. The newspaper of the Party announced that, "those who protest against the removal of the Swabians were following a wrong path . . . those who hinder the removal weaken democracy."[23] The leaders of the Smallholder Party, on the other hand, tried to hinder the deportation of those Germans who were faithful to the cause of Hungary in the past years. Non-Communist newspapers, like *Magyar Nemzet,* revealed anomalies and abuses committed in the course of the expulsions.

When Ferenc Nagy became Prime Minister on February 1, 1946, he intended to change the decree of December 22, 1945, on the point that individual guilt should be the basis for deportations. The Communist Party, however, opposed, and General Sviridov, acting chairman of the ACC, vetoed such modification. Eventually, as a compromise solution, the Minister of Interior issued instructions which aimed at the exemption of those individuals who spoke German as their mother tongue but declared themselves of Hungarian nationality in the census of 1941 and did not take part in any kind of pro-Nazi activities.

In practice neither the decree nor the instructions proved to be conclusive. The removals were carried out under the direction of the Ministry of Interior, that is, under Communist control. Miners and other skilled workers necessary for the economy of the country were exempted without much ado. Otherwise Communist dominated local committees granted exemptions according to postwar party affiliations. Patriotic merits of the past were given little consideration. Wealthy people especially were in a bad position because their property was wanted. Smallholder politicians intervened energetically for loyal Germans and such actions met with success in some cases but on the whole the procedure was in many places rather a caricature of justice.

Following American protests, the German deportations to the United States zone were discontinued on June 1, 1946, then reassumed and then definitively stopped by the end of 1946. It was characteristic of the Communist attitude in Hungary that the Communist Minister of Interior, László Rajk, complained in July, 1946, because of the suspension of the expatriations by the American authorities. He advocated the necessity of continuing the expulsions and argued that there was a land shortage and that the properties of the German expellees were needed for the Hungarians who were to be removed from Czechoslovakia.[24] Thus Rajk played directly into the hands of the Czechoslovaks and Russians who at the peace negotiations connected the removal of the Hungarians from Czechoslovakia with the removal of the Germans from Hungary while Hungarian foreign policy opposed such a combination. Thanks to the support of the peace delegation of the United States, Hungarian diplomacy in Paris defeated this Communist maneuver.

According to the memoirs of General Clay, the United States zone of Germany received altogether 168,000 expellees from Hungary.[25] In an official publication, the American Military Governor put their number at 175,591.[26] A statement made in the Hungarian National Assembly estimated the number to be 157,000.[27] The census taken in Western Germany on September 13, 1950, showed 178,100 Germans originating from Hungary,[28] but this number also includes the Swabians who took refuge in Germany before the expulsion began.

Since the American zone was not willing to accept German expellees after 1946, deportations were continued during 1947 and 1948 to the Russian zone of Germany. In this second phase of deportations many more abuses were committed than in 1946. Some Hungarian newspapers gave accurate accounts of these abuses.[29] According to the estimate of German refugee organizations about 50,000 Germans were removed to Eastern Germany. Thus the number of German expellees from Hungary was somewhat over 200,000, but this figure is certainly less than half of the 500,000 authorized by the Allied Control Council for Germany.

An interplay of actions and circumstances hindered an all out expulsion of the Germans from Hungary. In 1945, the Smallholder Party and the Hungarian Foreign Ministry delayed preparations as much as was possible under the circumstances. In the following year the policy of the United States began to change, and as noted above, the United States zone ceased to accept expellees by the end of 1946. The absorbing capacity of the Russian zone was limited, and later Russian policy toward the Germans also underwent a change.

In addition to the deportations, the German minority group in Hungary suffered other losses. As mentioned, the Red Army deported Germans from Hungary, and several thousand Germans left Hungary with the retreating German Army. Some of the Germans remained in Austria or emigrated overseas. The total number of Germans in Hungary was probably diminished by about 230,000–250,000.

During the transfer, the Catholic Bishops of Hungary expressed the opinion of the Hungarian public when they energetically protested against the indiscriminate expulsion of the Germans.[30] Joseph Cardinal Mindszenty took a stand against collective punishment of the Swabians in a pastoral letter of October 17, 1945, and in forceful terms, repeatedly expressed the same views. When the deportations of the Germans to the Russian zone of Germany were continued in 1947, the Catholic hierarchy renewed the protests. The Bishops addressed a collective letter to Prime Minister Lajos Dinnyés on August 8, 1947,[31] and later Cardinal Mindszenty issued a pastoral letter in the name of the Hungarian Bishops against the forcible transfer of the Germans and Magyars.[32]

The repeated protestations of the Catholic hierarchy were considered by the Communist Party as treacherous actions. But Communist policy is a changing pattern and promptly follows the transformations of the Moscow line. Thus, in 1948, Hungary suspended expatriation of German-speaking Hungarians; and announcements were made concerning the equality of Germans with other Hungarian citizens. This new policy was implemented in March, 1950, when the Hungarian Government issued a decree under which Germans expelled from Hungary after the war were authorized to return and all German inhabitants of Hungary received fully guaranteed equal rights.[33] Actually, as Annabring pointed out, up to 1948, many German expellees were anxious to return to Hungary and made great sacrifices to prove their loyalty and to qualify for exemption. However, after Communist domination was fully established in Hungary, they were glad to be in Western Germany and desperately tried to bring their relatives out of Hungary.[34]

Although legal discrimination against the Germans in Hungary was abolished, restitution of lost properties did not follow. Communist-dominated Hungarian foreign policy further changed its course to conform to that of Moscow. In October, 1952, Prime Minister Mátyás Rákosi, accompanied by other cabinet members, paid an official visit to East Germany where he was received with full military honors. Rákosi reviewed solemn military parades, and both the German and Hungarian Communist leaders emphasized the traditional "everlasting" and "indissoluble" Hungarian-German friendship. Among the troops marching before the Hungarian Communist leaders may have been some of the Germans expelled from Hungary as Nazis. Notwithstanding such trifles, State Minister Ernö Gerö declared during the visit that the Germans and Hungarians would march together, not for one year or two, but forever. Thus the political pendulum of the Communist policy in Hungary completed a full swing on the German question. This change, however, did not improve the heavy lot of the Swabians. As an observer, I can only conclude that the story of the expulsion of the Germans from Hungary is a dismal chapter in postwar diplomacy.

NOTES

1. Large groups of Germans settled in Hungary as early as the twelfth and thirteenth centuries. These early settlements came into being in Transylvania and in Northern Hungary, territories attached by the Treaty of Trianon to Rumania and Czechoslovakia. Under King Matthias, at the end of the fifteenth century, Hungary had a population of approximately five millions, of which 75 to 80 percent were Magyars. During the Turkish wars and occupation, battles were fought for nearly two centuries on the plains and in the hill districts, which regions were densely populated by the Magyars. Consequently, centers of Hungarian culture were annihilated in vast areas. After the expulsion of the Turks, a census in 1720 revealed only three and a half million persons in Hungary proper. Subsequently, the Imperial Gov-

ernment of Vienna directed a large-scale colonization, which diminished the proportion of the Magyars even more. Immigrants came from all over Europe. The majority consisted of Germans, Rumanians and Slovaks from Northern Hungary, but also included were French, Alsatian, Catalan, Italian, Dutch, Bulgarian, Armenian and other settlers. The overwhelming part of the German minority that lived in post First World War Hungary had moved into the country in the course of this eighteenth century colonization period, that is, they lived for more than two centuries in Hungary.

As to conditions in Hungary after the expulsion of the Turks, see Henry Marczali, *Hungary in the Eighteenth Century,* with an introductory essay on the earlier history of Hungary by Harold W. V. Temperley (Cambridge, 1910). Cf. Count Paul Teleki, *The Evolution of Hungary and Its Place in European History* (New York, 1923), pp. 54–87. For the changes of Hungary's population, see *The Hungarian Peace Negotiations,* Vol. I. published by the Royal Hungarian Ministry of Foreign Affairs, (Budapest, 1921), pp. 43–53.

2. For the developments in Yugoslavia and Rumania, see Joseph B. Schechtman, "The Elimination of German Minorities in Southeastern Europe," *Journal of Central European Affairs,* 6 (1946), 152–162. *Men Without the Rights of Man, A Report on the Expulsion and Extermination of German Speaking Minority Groups in the Balkans and Prewar Poland,* published by the Committee Against Mass Expulsion (New York, 1947).

3. These questions were debated in the Hungarian press. *Szabad Szó,* the organ of the National Peasant Party, and the Communist Party organ, *Szabad Nép,* advocated the wholesale deportation of the Germans as early as April and May, 1945. See, especially *Szabad Szó,* April 22, 1945. For the more moderate views, see *Magyar Nemzet,* May 1, 8, 12, 16, 1945. Some politicians advocated an internal dispersion of the Germans in order to dissolve the compact German settlements in Hungary.

4. Ferenc Erdei was a member of the Peasant Party, but actually he owed exclusive allegiance to the Communist Party and fulfilled Communist orders.

5. The American memorandum dealt with the possible expulsion of Magyars from Rumania, Yugoslavia and Czechoslovakia and noted, "The Governments of those states are primarily concerned with the matter of responsibility of these Hungarians for crimes against the state of which such Hungarians are citizens. The United States Government, however, would not consider it justified to deal with all members of an ethnic group who constitute a minority as criminals against the state and as subject to expulsion from its territory, only

because of their ethnic origin." *Hungary at the Conference of Paris,* Vol. II (Budapest, 1947), pp. 4–5.

6. "The three governments having considered the question in all its aspects, recognize that the transfer to Germany of German populations, or elements thereof, remaining in Poland, Czechoslovakia and Hungary, will have to be undertaken. They agree, that any transfers that take place should be effected in an orderly and humane manner.

"Since the influx of a large number of Germans into Germany would increase the burden already resting on the occupying authorities, they consider that the Allied Control Council in Germany should in the first instance examine the problem with special regard to the question of the equitable distribution of these Germans among the several zones of occupation. They are accordingly instructing their respective representatives on the Control Council to report to their governments as soon as possible the extent to which such persons have already entered Germany from Poland, Czechoslovakia and Hungary, and to submit an estimate of the time and rate at which further transfers could be carried out, having regard to the present situation in Germany.

"The Czechoslovak Government, the Polish Provisional Government and the Control Council in Hungary are at the same time being informed of the above, and are being requested meanwhile to suspend further expulsions pending the examination by the Governments concerned of the report from their representatives on the Control Council." *Department of State Bulletin,* XIII (1945), 160.

7. 81st Congress, 2d Session, Report No. 1841.

8. *Ibid.,* p. 6. This report described the motives behind the American position at Potsdam in the following way: "Premier Stalin himself is the principal source for the information that large-scale expulsions took place long before Potsdam. As early as the Yalta Conference, in February 1945, he had said, 'Where our troops come in, the Germans run away.' At Potsdam during the meeting of July 25, 1945, he stated that Poland had already expelled millions of Germans and that, although one and a half million remained, these were being held only to help with the harvest. Then they, too, would be expelled. He remarked that the Czechs were giving the Germans two hours' notice in which to move out. Premier Stalin emphasized that nothing could be done to stop these expulsions. He felt that not only the Big Three but the Polish and Czech Governments themselves were powerless to prevent the process, which was occurring because of deep-rooted and bitter feelings of the people against the Germans.

"It was against this background of the accomplished fact of large-scale expulsions, coupled with Soviet unwillingness to do anything about them, that the United States sponsorship of article XIII must be considered. Granted that nothing could be done to stop the expulsions altogether, the United States was anxious to do everything possible to improve the situation. We therefore sponsored article XIII of the Potsdam agreement because it was the best that could be done at the time to prevent further inhumanity and disorder in the transfers. When article XIII was considered on the July 31, 1945, meeting at Potsdam, Premier Stalin objected on the ground that it would do no good—the Polish and Czech Governments would go right on expelling Germans, no matter what the Potsdam agreement said. The United States, however, continued to urge approval of article XIII. Secretary of State Byrnes said that article XIII would not completely solve the German expellee problem, but would at least slow up the wholesale expulsion of Germans then in progress. Premier Stalin then reluctantly agreed to include article XIII in the Potsdam agreement.

"*From this, it is apparent that the United States certainly was not responsible at Potsdam for encouraging or authorizing the expulsion of Germans from eastern Europe. Expulsions had been going on long before Potsdam; we were merely trying to do all that was possible to make this process more orderly and humane.*"

9. The decision of the Allied Control Council was published in Washington on December 7, 1945. This press release of the State Department pointed out that it was the purpose of the Allied Control Council, "to do what it can to see that the transfers are effected in an orderly and humane manner in accordance with the Potsdam agreement. Many Germans have already migrated into Germany from Poland and from territory now under Polish administration, often under conditions which made very difficult the orderly settlement of the persons involved. The present decision of the Allied Control Council should greatly alleviate those difficulties. Before the Potsdam conference the Czecho-Slovak Government had determined to transfer a substantial part of the German minority in Czechoslovakia to Germany. The decisions of the Potsdam Conference and of the Allied Control Council should help to ensure that these transfers will be carried out as humanely as possible." *Department of State Bulletin,* XIII (1945), 937.

10. The pertinent parts of General W. S. Key's diary and his comments were put at the disposal of the writer through the courtesy of General Key and are used with his authorization.

11. The Germans in Hungary usually are called Swabians.

12. For the full text of this note, see Stephen Kertesz, *Diplomacy in a Whirlpool: Hungary between Nazi Germany and the Soviet Union,* (Notre Dame, Publication date August, 1953). Document No. 10.

13. The Hungarians in Czechoslovakia outnumbered the Slovaks in Hungary at least seven to one. Thus, even after a total exchange of Slovaks for Hungarians there would have remained more than half a million Hungarians in Slovakia. Hence, the total expulsion of the Germans from Hungary was offered as a handy solution. For the Prague negotiations, see *Hungary and the Conference of Paris,* Vol. II (Budapest, 1947), pp. 30–53.

14. President Beneš was probably misinformed about the intentions of the Western powers. Otherwise it would be difficult to understand why he later reiterated the statement made to Gyöngyösi in an article in which Beneš explained: "The choice is between the concept of a national state and the formerly recognized Wilsonian concept of a state of nationalities, with all that involves. In a national state there is no room for minority problems. The rule applies just as much to the Germans as to the Hungarians in Czechoslovakia; and it concerns not only Czechoslovakia but also Hungary, Yugoslavia, Rumania and Poland. *Even the Great Powers have recognized that in the interest of peace in Europe there remains no other solution but the removal of the Germans and Hungarians from Czechoslovakia. The Potsdam Conference solemnly and definitely recognized this principle and notified the Czechoslovak Government of it.* [Italics added]. Poland and Hungary were also notified by the Powers of their decision in regard to Germans living in their territory, and both of them accepted this essential change." Eduard Beneš, "Postwar Czechoslovakia," *Foreign Affairs,* 24 (April, 1946), 400–401.

Since the Czechoslovak policy aiming at the expulsion of the Hungarians from Czechoslovakia met with American resistance, the expulsion of the Germans from Hungary might have been offered by the Soviet Union as a substitute and an indirect solution of the problem. The Western acceptance of this Soviet proposal at Potsdam was probably the basis of President Beneš' information. The present writer knows through personal experience that the British Ambassador to Czechoslovakia supported Beneš' policy and advocated the total removal of the Hungarians from Czechoslovakia. British diplomacy in Budapest was unresponsive in the matter.

15. "The United States Mission in Hungary presents its compliments to the Ministry for Foreign Affairs and wishes to inform the Hungarian Government that the United States Government has been seriously perturbed by reports of continued mass movements of German refugees who presumably have been summarily expelled from their homes and dispossessed of all property except that which they can carry. These German refugees, who appear to have entered Germany from areas east of the Oder-Neisse Line, are mostly women, children and

old people, who have arrived in a shocking state of exhaustion, in many cases robbed of all their few personal possessions and ill with contagious diseases. The Potsdam Agreement states in paragraph 13 that the transfer of population shall be conducted in an orderly and humane manner. Consequently, such mass distress and maltreatment of the weak and helpless is at variance with this agreement as it also is with international standards for the treatment of refugees."

16. This *Note Verbale* was addressed to the British and United States Political Missions in Budapest. For its text, see Stephen Kertesz, *op. cit.,* Document 11. It was thought necessary to urge explicitly a reply to the problems exposed in the note of December 1, 1945, because the victorious powers were usually slow in answering Hungarian notes if they reacted to them at all. For example, in the case of the persecution of the Hungarians in Czechoslovakia, the Hungarian Government addressed 184 notes to the ACC between April, 1945 and July, 1946. No action or even answer resulted. As the persecutions continued, the Hungarian Government repeatedly sent complaints accompanied by extensive memorandums directly to the British, American and Soviet representatives in Budapest. In a note of September 12, 1945, the Hungarian Government requested a hearing by the Council of Allied Foreign Ministers on the question of the Hungarians in Czechoslovakia, and proposed that an international commission of inquiry, composed of the representatives of France, Great Britain, the Soviet Union and the United States, should investigate and examine the controversial issues between Hungary and Czechoslovakia. This request was reiterated in another note of November 20, 1945, when the Hungarian Government asked that the districts of Slovakia inhabited by Hungarians be placed under international control, pending the appointment of the commission of inquiry. To these and to some other proposals the Russians did not react, and the entirely negative American and British replies arrived in February and March, 1946. For the text of the pertinent notes, see *Hungary and the Conference of Paris,* Vol. II (Budapest, 1947), pp. 13–29, 50–55, 155–163.

17. Concerning the various endeavors of the Smallholder Party aiming at the limitation of the expulsion to those Germans who were guilty as individuals, see Ferenc Nagy, *The Struggle Behind the Iron Curtain* (New York, 1948), pp. 131–132, 168–169, 198–202.

According to the Smallholder proposals, the Germans to be expelled would have been restricted to those who (1) declared themselves of German vernacular *and* of German nationality at the last census, (2) changed back their Magyarized names into German, (3) voluntarily joined the German army, (4) were members of the *Volksbund.* In some of these categories the element of "guilt" was based on presumptions which were not always correct. At the same time, however, the proven anti-Nazi Germans would have been exempted from transfer in all categories. Whatever the shortcomings of this system, it offered some possibility of restricting deportations. In 1939, the Ministry of Interior authorized the *Volksbund* as a cultural association of the Germans in Hungary, which, however, gradually became the center of pro-Nazi activities.

18. For the text of this memorandum, see S. Kertesz, *op. cit.,* Document 21.

19. *Hungary and the Conference of Paris,* Vol. IV (Budapest, 1947) pp. 77–78. The peace delegation of Hungary opposed, and after a hard struggle, defeated the Czechoslovak proposal aiming at the expulsion of 200,000 Hungarians. This was the only instance at the Paris Conference in which a state under the occupation of the Red Army openly opposed a move sponsored by the USSR and asked for Western political support. This opposition, however, would have been futile without the energetic support of the United States delegation.

   "Mr. Smith," mentioned by Vyshinsky, is General Walter Bedell Smith. At that time he was the American Ambassador to the Soviet Union and the representative of the American peace delegation in the Territorial and Political Commission for Hungary.

20. The expulsion of the Germans from Hungary is described in detail with most of the pertinent decrees and other official texts by Matthias Annabring, "Das ungarländische Deutschtum, Leidensweg einer südostdeutschen Volksgruppe," *Südost-Stimmen,* II, Sondernummer (March, 1952), 1–80.

21. Lucius D. Clay, *Decision in Germany* (New York, 1950), pp. 313–314. In January, 1946, the Hungarian Government concluded an agreement with the United States military authorities in Germany which regulated the transfer procedure.

22. The relevant experiences were summed up in the following way:

   "It is a fact, however, that by and large the Hungarian Government proceeded less ruthlessly against the German minority than any other Soviet satellite. Attempts were made, however crude and imperfect, to distinguish between magyarized Swabians and others. The expellees were allowed to take more property with them than similar groups in Poland, Yugoslavia, Czechoslovakia, or Rumania. Fewer people perished in 'work camps' than in neighboring countries. Even so, the record is shocking, and at least once the American Military Government felt constrained to refuse the acceptance into Germany of further refugee trains because of the deplorable conditions prevailing in these transports." *Men Without the Rights of Man,* p. 11.

The American-licensed German newspaper *Neckarzeitung* in its issue of June 19, 1946, gave the following description: "Hungary is making rapid progress in the expulsion of Germans. Except for the arbitrary actions of those detailed to escort the refugee transports, the letter of the law is generally obeyed. Except for activists interned in work camps, hardly any Germans who registered as members of the *Volksbund* in 1941 are allowed to remain in the country. The refugees are arriving in fair health. The expellees from Hungary have more baggage than those from other countries: one hundred kilograms, including food. They have bedding, kitchen utensils, and some clothing besides what they wear. The ages range from the youngest to the very old. Families are often not complete. The present whereabouts of sons who were in the war are usually not known. In the absence of adult males, young women were drafted for work in Russia. A few have returned; others hope to go from Russia directly back to Germany, at some future date." The English translation of this article was published in *Men Without the Rights of Man,* p. 10.

23 *Szabad Nép,* January 19, 1946.
24. *Szabad Nép,* July 14, 1946. The Hungarian Ministry of Interior negotiated with the representatives of the U.S. Military Government in Germany concerning the resumption of the transfers. These negotiations were successfully concluded on August 22, 1946 and were made public on August 31. The time and manner of the publication of this agreement was most inopportune for the Hungarian peace delegation, which was under pressure in Paris to accept the removal of 200,000 Hungarians from Czechoslovakia.
25. Clay, *op. cit.,* p. 314.
26. *Monthly Report of the Military Governor.* Office of the Military Government for Germany (U.S.) 1–31 July, 1947. Statistical Annex, p. 4. Earlier reports in 1947, mentioned higher figures, amounting to 180,000.
27. *Szabad Nép,* February 17, 1948.
28. Annabring, *op. cit.,* p. 60.
29. See, for example, the articles published in the *Ellenzék,* October 4, 1947, and *Hazánk,* October 17, 1947. The Catholic episcopate and Cardinal Mindszenty also described the various evil practices. Cf. below footnotes 31 and 32.
30. 83.3 percent of the Swabians were Catholics: in the countryside the percentage of the Catholics among them was 84.9 percent and in the cities 67 percent. The rest of the Swabians were Protestants: 13.9 percent Lutherans and 1.8 percent Calvinists.
31. The collective letter stated: "The Bishops of Hungary are greatly alarmed by the news that the expulsion of the German minority is to

be continued. In 1944 we did our utmost to prevent the Government then in power from carrying out the inhuman deportation of the Jews. Conscious of the mission entrusted to us by God, we consider it now our duty to protest against the expulsion of the German-speaking minority. The more so since they are of our faith.

"We have already lodged a protest with your predecessor in office. For we would have no right to be indignant about the cruel expulsion of the Hungarians from Czechoslovakia if we approved of the self-same methods being employed in our own country where the Germans have been settled for more than two hundred years.

"We protested against measures of this kind when the whole of the German minority was to be made collectively responsible for the treacherous actions of such groups as the *Volksbund* and the SS. We protested against a practice that punished with the traitors not only innocent and politically indifferent people, but also those very people who had avowedly professed their loyalty to the Hungarian homeland by supporting the 'Loyalty Movement' even when they did not wish to forego their mother-tongue." *Authorized White Book Cardinal Mindszenty Speaks* (New York, 1949), pp. 139-140.

32. The pastoral letter of October 2, 1947, pointed out the most salient injustices and abuses practiced in the course of the deportation procedures in the following way:

"Not only those persons whose great-grandmothers on their mother's side were of Magyar stock and, on their father's side, descended from Alsatian stock, but even those who can prove their Magyar descent on both sides are being expelled. Nor is any consideration paid to those who professed themselves Magyars in the days of Hitler and who were consequently persecuted by the Germans. Their children do not even know a word of German.

"No regard is paid to family bonds. Children are lost because their mothers are unable to look after them in the general confusion of the hasty departure. We do not need, however, to expatiate on details . . .

"One possibility, however, of remaining in this country is left to these unhappy people, a most illuminating feature which throws light on the whole situation. If a man declares his willingness to give up his property and hand it over to some stranger who, in return, is prepared to vouch for him, he is allowed to stay in this country. Does this make such a man any less a German? Is he no longer considered a danger to Hungary?

"A dreadful story is thus disclosed. All this goes on in this age of humanity, of human dignity, of freedom and of the establishment of a happier and more *democratic* life! We cannot refrain from crying out loudly against these things." *Ibid.,* pp. 146-147.

33. *New York Times,* April 2, 1950. Cf. Annabring, *op. cit.,* pp. 70–71.
34. Annabring, *op. cit.,* pp. 74–75.